EVEN AT THE GRAVE

EVEN
AT THE
GRAVE

LISA G. SAUNDERS

MCP

Mill City Press, Inc.
2301 Lucien Way #415
Maitland, FL 32751
407.339.4217
www.millcitypress.net

Printed in the United States of America

ISBN-13: 978-1-54561-921-6

CONTENTS

—§—

For Tim, who even loves me.

ACKNOWLEDGMENTS

To Chip Edens, who practically insisted I write something and gave me the confidence to try.

To my editors: Doug Mays, who slogged through the first drafts and made me realize what an editor offers; Chris Martin, who helping me to write more with fewer words; Ken Garfield, who improved flow and content: and Geoff Smith, my hero, who pruned and polished; to my proofreader, Meredith Tennant; and Phillip Gessart for the cover and interior design.

To my early readers, who provided encouragement and valuable suggestions: Lisa Ugland, Jeanne Kutrow, Jane Showalter, Gail Landers, Missy Miller, Lynn Tate, Anne Middleton, Sandy Cummings, Sandra Griffin, Rachel Williams, Ben Hill, Kathy Hill, Patty Rhyne, Kimberly Lakin, Carrington Coulter, Jane Coulter, Lois Ann Partridge, Marian Wright, Zeta Pittman, Amanda and Terry Robertson, and my sisters, Ginny Jenkins and Cobey Wagoner.

To all the families who gave me permission to tell the story of their loved ones.

To Julie Marr, who suggested I have introductory quotes for each chapter.

To Kathy Izard, who inspired me to keep rewriting and not give up too early.

To my husband, Tim, and our children, Caroline, Julia Gray and Rob, who cheer me on along the way, never squawk about being sermon or book fodder, and fill my life with joy.

—§—

Tom's secretary recalls being worried when she first started working for him. As she put it, Tom had a "gorgeous" education from Virginia and Harvard, and she had a high school diploma. But Tom always treated her with respect and kindness. Each morning, as bank president, Tom greeted everyone by name and with a cheery "Good morning." He expected a good day's work out of everyone, but he was also interested in people's personal well-being, writing beautiful notes to colleagues and employees who suffered loss or hardship. When his secretary's mother was ill, Tom told her, "I want you to know that your family comes first. If you need to leave, just go." At her mother's nursing home, she discovered that Tom had been by to pay her mother a visit. He had never mentioned he was going.

FROM THE HOMILY PREACHED AT THE FUNERAL FOR TOM STORRS

CHAPTER 1
STOPPING TIME

I don't remember anything about the first funeral I attended. It was for my grandfather, Robert Goodwin Sr., and I was four. The story goes that when I saw my grandmother crying, I proclaimed, loud enough for all to hear, "Let's dig him up."

My mother's family had a tradition to stop a clock at a death. An ivory porcelain timepiece painted with pink and lavender flowers sat silent on a table in our living room. Its hands were stilled when my mother's Aunt CeCe died. I never knew her. And I don't know the time of her death, because as a child I would pry open the clock's glass face and twirl the hands round and round.

Funerals, however, do stop time. Work is abandoned, plans are undone. But funerals also create time: time for reflection, connection, and appreciation. As a priest in the Episcopal Church, I have officiated at hundreds of funerals. I knew that would be part of the package. I didn't know they would be so formative, rewarding, and inspiring. Funerals—the lead up, the events themselves, and what follows—usually provide me a front row seat to profound courage as well as heartbreak. But most of all I am a witness to hope and the enduring, renewing power of love.

The defining moment of my religion takes place in a cemetery. So it should not be surprising that the ground of hope is never firmer than when standing at the grave of a loved one.

Priests are expected to hatch, match, and dispatch. Presiding at baptisms and weddings is joyous. But it is the dispatches—the funerals—that pick me up by the lapels and loosen what's too tight and tighten what's too loose. I am set back down realigned and grateful.

I presided at my first funeral for a man I had never met.

It started with a call from a funeral home director while I was working at St. Philip's Episcopal Church in Coral Gables, Florida.

"Would you be available to offer a graveside burial?" the director asked. "It was the deceased's request that the service be conducted from the Episcopal Book of Common Prayer, but he was not a member of a church here."

"Yes, I can do that," I replied. It was not how I expected my first funeral to play out, but it would be good practice. "Can you give me the contact information for the man's family?"

He cleared his throat. "His family doesn't live here, and none will be present for the burial."

No family attending. Odd, I thought. He must be an old bachelor. "Did he have any children?" I asked to confirm my deduction.

"No."

As I suspected. "How old was he?"

"The deceased was thirty-one."

I wasn't prepared for that answer.

"Good heavens!" I said. "So young ... what happened to him?"

There was a pause.

"He was sick." Another pause. "The fact of the matter is he died of AIDS."

I hadn't even thought of that possibility. The year was 1985. AIDS had only recently been identified.

"You may not see this much at your church, but we do all the time here now. Young men dying whose families don't want anything to do with them on account of AIDS. Some guys come in and pay for their funeral in advance. Some make special requests about the service, like this man did, but most just ask for the cheapest options."

Looking back, I absorbed the tragedy of this young man's story, but not its depth. I was twenty-six years old. The sort of forsakenness that he must have suffered was completely foreign to me.

The funeral home director picked me up in a hearse later that week. He recruited cemetery employees to carry the casket to the gravesite. The sun, as it often is in Miami, was relentless. We stood beside the casket, dripping, I in my vestments and the funeral director in his black suit.

"All we go down to the dust," I read from the Book of Common Prayer burial service. "Yet even at the grave we make our song: alleluia, alleluia, alleluia."

We were there to see a man's body lowered into the grave. What he needed even more was for us to uphold his dignity.

I received two more calls from the same funeral home that year. Identical circumstances. Each young man was buried without a friend or family member present, as if he were a criminal.

No, I take that back. Even the families of criminals show up at the grave.

On November 25, 1963, President John F. Kennedy was buried at Arlington National Cemetery. The stylish and stoic Jackie Kennedy, dressed in widow's black, with young Caroline and little John-John saluting his father's casket are familiar images of history. While most of our nation gathered around the television to mourn our president's death, at the very same hour Kennedy's assassin, Lee Harvey Oswald, was being buried at a cemetery in Fort Worth, Texas. Oswald's immediate family attended the service, as well as a slew of journalists, photographers, police, and federal officials. My husband's uncle, the Reverend Louis Saunders, was also present. Though he didn't plan on it, Uncle Louis wound up presiding at Oswald's funeral.

Oswald was married to Marina, a young woman from Russia who was only twenty-two when her husband was shot by Jack Ruby two days after the assassination. The Oswalds had two daughters: June was twenty-one months at the time of the shooting, and Rachel was five weeks. Marina and the girls as well as Oswald's mother and brother were at the grave. But the Lutheran pastor who had agreed to preside at the service was a no-show.

The day before Oswald's funeral, Uncle Louis, in his capacity as the executive director of the Dallas–Fort Worth Council of Churches, called the funeral home where Oswald's body had been sent, asking if they had found a minister to officiate at the service. The funeral home assured him that a Lutheran pastor had been secured. But on the day of the funeral, instead of watching President Kennedy's flag-draped casket carried on a horse-drawn caisson, Uncle Louis's mind was on the cemetery where the Oswalds would gather. Feeling a responsibility for the area's religious community, he drove the thirty-two miles out to Shannon Rose Hill Cemetery in Fort Worth to be certain everything went as planned.

Just as he had feared, no minister appeared.

In addition, there were no pallbearers. Members of the press put down their notebooks and cameras and carried Oswald's casket to the grave. The funeral home director told Oswald's mother, Marguerite, that the Reverend Louis Saunders was present. She asked if Uncle Louis would preside at her son's service. He nodded in agreement and with no preparation for his footnote in history, he walked up to the grave and took on the task of pastoring to the family of the most despised man in America.

He recited Psalm 23 and John 14 from memory. He said that they were there to bury Oswald and not to judge him.

"Mrs. Oswald tells me that her son, Lee Harvey, was a good boy and that she loved him. And today, Lord, we commit his spirit to your divine care."

With that, Oswald's eulogy was over and done.

Marina, Oswald's wife, began calling Uncle Louis. Distraught and weeping, she sought comfort from her lonely nightmare. The Secret Service provided protection for Uncle Louis after he received death threats. When he died at age eighty-eight in 1998, an article ran in the *New York Times* remembering him for officiating at Oswald's funeral. Fifteen years later, when no pastor would step up to bury one of the accused bombers of the Boston Marathon, Uncle Louis's story was lifted up again in newspapers as an example of human decency and Christian charity.

One of the most humbling privileges of officiating at a funeral is to be permitted for a time into a family's intimate circle at a vulnerable moment. To think that I might be able to offer some sort of comfort, strength, or hope—or unintentionally deepen their pain—makes me feel vulnerable too.

For those young men I buried in Miami, two strangers became their family at the last: a rookie priest who could not fathom their pain and an undertaker who had seen too much of it. I regret today that I did not weep for them.

I look at the photograph of Uncle Louis with the Oswald family and wonder how it felt to be included in that family's circle. I hope that they drew solace from Uncle Louis's willingness to join their broken, reviled ranks. I hope that his presence—how he sat down beside them and didn't run off as soon as his task was complete—made them feel something that would thereafter elude them for years: a measure of respect and kindness.

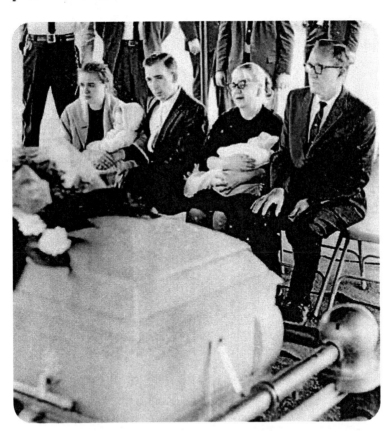

From left: Lee Harvey Oswald's wife, Marina, holding June; his brother, Robert; his mother, Marguerite, holding Rachel; and the Reverend Louis Saunders, my husband's uncle.

—§—

An only child, Frank said that no kid should grow up alone, so he
filled his house with children. His oldest child remembers Frank
reading the tales of King Arthur at bedtime. When the youngest
was in kindergarten, Frank, perhaps weary of children's stories,
tucked him in while reading the World War II story THEY WERE
EXPENDABLE. *Frank never talked down to his children. He*
encouraged and inspired them. They remember their very proper
father singing tender lullabies. Frank didn't yell or fool around
with things like time-out either. He had a look that sufficed on its
own. He was a man it felt worse to disappoint than disobey.

FROM THE HOMILY PREACHED AT THE FUNERAL FOR
FRANK THIES

CHAPTER 2
DAD GIVE AWAY

I t's not hard to describe my dad. It's hard to *stop* describing him.
My father likes to say and do things that draw attention, or at
the very least create conversation—like wearing a black armband when
his oldest daughter turned thirteen, or flustering left-handed waiters
and receptionists by saying, "I see you are a sinistral person," or taking
tap dance lessons in his fifties. He is also the man who came home
from work every day and gave his wife a big kiss with exaggerated
smacking noises as if he had been waiting all day to do just that, who
got up every Sunday morning and went to church with his family, who
helped pay the college tuition of his hairdresser's daughter. I can see
him sitting at his mammoth oak desk and hear the check for the Sunday offering plate ripped out of the ledger just before we head out
the door.

I was fifteen at the first funeral I remember attending. I went with
Dad. Just the two of us. I didn't know the deceased, but her framed
photograph sits in my house today.

Dad was a big man for most of his life, 6'2", 250 pounds—or an
eighth of a ton, as he liked to say. He still loves to make people laugh,
knows the art of a good story, and takes great delight when someone
manages to get his goat. He taught English at North Forsyth High
School where students came from towns called Tobaccoville and Rural

Hall. But they were no rubes. When an education professor came to observe him in the classroom, Dad announced that the class had a visitor. "He has come to watch a master teacher at work," Dad quipped. The class sat stone still. Then a petite blonde in the back of the room raised her hand.

"Yes?" Dad asked.

"Mr. Goodwin," she asked with a straight face, "does this mean we won't be playing Bingo today?"

Dad loved telling that story.

My parents were twenty and twenty-one when they married in 1951 at St. Mary's School chapel in Raleigh. Three days later, knowing that his draft notice was in the mail, Dad cut short their honeymoon in Myrtle Beach and enlisted in the army. Though he graduated from college with an English degree, he was assigned to the Army Finance Corps and never saw combat or went overseas.

After four years of service, Dad sold life insurance in his hometown to support his young family. He volunteered to teach classes for salesmen who needed to pass their Chartered Life Underwriter exam. He said some of his students could barely pass water. Yet his students scored better than any others in the state. He was asked to teach more classes and achieved similar results. Then Dad's mother died suddenly, six months after his father's death (my grandfather of the "dig him up" story).

My father's parents were in their sixties, and as their only child, he was very close to them. Their deaths, so near to one another, crushed him. The loss altered Dad's career path, which in turn made possible the most fortuitous decision of my life.

He reenrolled as a full-time student at the University of North Carolina. He was assigned a dorm room and a freshman roommate. My father was thirty-five years old, married, with three little girls back at home. He had the time of his life eating at his old fraternity house each day and as the only male student in education classes full of young women.

Teaching high school English proved to be a perfect fit for Dad's personality and gifts. Adept at flying by the seat of his pants, he mastered the vagaries of a classroom. He loved the brash freshness of teenagers, as well as discovering those wallflowers who blossomed under the light of a little well-deserved encouragement. Many of his students became the first in their families to go to college. Dad quickly realized that plenty of his students were smarter than he was, and he welcomed learning from them. His strategy was to teach to the brightest student in the class and let the others rise to the challenge.

Six times a day, a new audience was ushered into his room. It was well known that students who laughed at his jokes could earn a better grade. Every Friday he gave a vocabulary test, and the first and last words were always the same: *mundane* and *vicissitudes*. Yet the vicissitudes of his career were hardly mundane. Every day I watched Dad go to a job he loved. I thought everyone got to do that.

Dad's students read short stories by Willa Cather, Shirley Jackson, and Herman Melville. So I read them too, long before I was in high school. He taught *Macbeth*, *The Merchant of Venice*, Ralph Waldo Emerson's essays on self-reliance, and the Bible's Book of Job. Carl Sandburg entered Dad's classroom "on cat's paws." A unit on American artists ended with a test asking students to identify fifty classic paintings like *Whistler's Mother*, *Christina's World*, *Nighthawks*, *American Gothic*, and *Madame X*.

Dad held court for thirty-one years at the same school. An accomplished attorney and the former president of the North Carolina Bar Association told me that he owed his success to my father. As his teacher, Dad pushed him and prepared him to believe in himself and to dream bigger. I learned the same thing from a woman who said she was at the bottom of the class, but Dad kept bugging her to apply to college. He told her she wrote too well to settle for less. When I heard these stories, Dad was suffering with dementia, and they would make me cry. Few people still saw him as the dynamic teacher and mentor he once was.

While teaching, Dad served as the faculty sponsor for the Key Club, a boys' service organization at his school. Club members manned the concessions stand at football games. Dad let me come with him on Friday nights and help. I was twelve years old, and high schoolers seemed like gods. For the most part they treated me with benign neglect.

One boy, however, was nice. He talked to me, and we worked as a team, helping make change or grabbing a hot dog order for the other. He was sixteen, and probably the first sixteen-year-old boy who wasn't my cousin to talk to me. He was an excellent student, one of the few boys to earn an A in my father's class. He held a school record in track, his girlfriend was a pretty and popular cheerleader, and in his senior year he was elected student body president.

After graduation, he came by our house to visit Dad from time to time. He made a point to speak to me as well. I was rail thin with frizzy brown hair and braces. Boys didn't notice me. I had a huge crush on him.

In the middle of exams during his freshman year of college, the boy's mother died. His father had died when he was six years old, and he was an only child. Dad said that the administration and faculty had known that the boy had a difficult home life, but because he seemed no worse for wear, and because at that time folks didn't report such concerns to social services, nothing was investigated further. What they didn't know was that the boy's mother was an alcoholic whose boyfriend beat her regularly.

The weekend before she died, the boy came home from college and asked a police officer to accompany him. He assumed he would find his mother black and blue, as he usually did, and he would convince her to press charges. But that weekend she had no obvious bruises, and she got mad at him for involving the police. The next weekend, her boyfriend shot her.

Dad and I went to her funeral. I wore a mauve knit dress and signed my name in the guest book. I don't recall the church service, but I remember the cemetery. It was May. The grass was new and velvety. I can still see the boy seated in front of his mother's casket, his head in his hands as he cried.

Seven years later I married that boy.

October 1, 1977. My first date with Tim.

—§—

Cutter's name suited someone so adept with the blade. I don't think it's possible to overrate his raw talent as an artist. In high school he turned a four-foot block of mahogany into a blue heron that had legs no thicker than a pencil and a hundred individual feathers.

Michelangelo was once asked how he decided what to create. The artist replied, "I saw the angel in the stone and carved until I set him free." Similarly, Cutter had an eye for what could emerge from wood, and while he set free many a trout, grouse, angel, lion, and house wren, the work seemed to set him free as well.

FROM THE HOMILY PREACHED AT THE FUNERAL FOR
CUTTER DAVIS

CHAPTER 3
RED ROVER

Red Rover, Red Rover, send Lisa right over!
I let go of the hands on either side of me, flushing to hear my name called. Buttercups dot the Brunson Elementary School field between my team and the one thirty yards away. My classmates are like a line of cutout paper dolls daring me to break through. I look for the weakest link and take off. My legs churn and each footfall digs into the soft ground as I accelerate. They are a wall, their hands clamped around each other's wrists. Stronger boys stand beside smaller girls. I see them flinch just before I hurtle into their arms. If hands come undone, I take the spoils of victory and bring one of them back. If thwarted, I join them in defeat.

Tag. Hide and Seek. King of the Hill. Mother May I. Marco Polo.

Many children's games are about being tapped, discovered, called out, chosen. They foreshadow our adult strivings to make a name for ourselves. When young we play with the intensity of work. When older we look for ways to make work more like play.

In my line of work, ministers are "called." The word *vocation* is derived from the Latin word for *call*. A call can come through others, but its origin is assumed to be divine. Ministers are not the only people called into professions. For instance, I think my father was called to teaching.

My husband, Tim, grew up watching his parents suffer from diseases he could not heal. Childhood wounds chart career paths too. He is a doctor. It is his calling.

On a beautiful, warm Sunday morning in May 1981, we walked at our graduations from the University of North Carolina at Chapel Hill, his from medical school and mine from college. The next weekend we walked down the aisle. We were married in Winston-Salem at Tim's home church, First Christian. The priest at my Episcopal church officiated along with Tim's Uncle Louis. At the close of the service, the congregation sang a hymn with the refrain, "Give us wisdom, give us courage, for the facing of this hour."

I knew I was marrying a doctor on my wedding day. Tim, however, had no idea he would soon be sleeping with a priest.

I was clueless too. People like me did not go into the ministry. That was for the Sam Warners of the world. Everyone in our third-grade class knew Sam would be a minister. Even at eight he was clean-cut, eager to please, risk averse, and a perfectionist. Sam beautifully pastors a Presbyterian church today. No one pegged me for the same. Besides, I wanted to be an actress.

I played Aunt Polly in a fourth-grade production of *Tom Sawyer* and the title role in fifth grade's *Sacajawea*. In sixth grade I was a convincing Lady Macbeth, rubbing my murderous hands with the lines, "Out, damned spot! Out, I say!" My mother sewed a velvet robe with fake white ermine trim for the part.

I liked performing and storytelling, and it turned out that church offered me outlets for this interest. Our parents took my two sisters and me to St. Timothy's Episcopal Church in Winston-Salem every Sunday, but I was the only one who got involved outside of the pew. I sang in the choir, entertained two-year-olds at Sunday school, served as an acolyte at the altar, and was president of the youth group. I played Lucy Fairweather, the heroine in our church's biannual melodrama, *Dark Deeds on the Diamond.*

Drama kick-started my interest in the Bible too. On a sleepover at my cousin Elizabeth's house in Charlotte, North Carolina, when I was twelve, I watched with fascination as she settled a heavy Bible on her lap and read quietly. Next, she set the Bible on her nightstand and knelt by her bed in prayer. The next Christmas I asked for a Bible and started at the beginning. There was enough sex in Genesis to keep me interested.

In middle and high school I wasn't cute enough to get lead parts in plays, and I couldn't carry a tune for musicals. I was cast as Princess #12 in *Once upon a Mattress* and Maid #2 in *Life with Father.*

I found a new role in Young Life, a nondenominational Christian outreach to teens. I joined a Bible study group when I was fifteen. I found Bible study to be relevant, absorbing, and challenging. Who knew that a letter written two thousand years ago could speak directly to a teenage girl's fears, or that the stories of Jesus in the Gospels had endless layers to peel back?

I developed a prayer life beyond Sunday morning and exam week. I shared my adolescent worries and hopes. If God was bored or bemused, I did not know it. Instead I sensed that God took joy in my prayers.

I read C.S. Lewis's classic, *Mere Christianity*, and got a charge out of theological gymnastics. My faith felt nimble and springy. Lewis wrote that God did not aim to make me nicer, but someone altogether new. He said the goal of the Christian life is "not like teaching a horse to jump better and better but like turning a horse into a winged creature."

Some might have foreseen my growing interest in spirituality as a sign predicting my future. But I didn't see it as having anything to do with a career.

In college I gave up on performing and turned to storytelling. I double majored in advertising and religion. I wrote ads for cereal and furniture polish, and a paper on Gideon's charge in the Book of Judges. Advertising taught me to hook a reader in the first line and move quickly and clearly to the point—excellent advice for any preacher.

I was a cub reporter for the *Winston-Salem Sentinel* for a summer in college. I pounded out articles on a manual typewriter. At lunchtime I walked a block to the white stone Centenary Methodist Church. The silent sanctuary felt more like home than the noisy newsroom. I had fifty bylines that summer, but *I* wasn't hooked. Good thing I had two majors.

I looked into postgraduate programs in religion because an undergraduate religion degree and a dollar can buy a cup of coffee. To be an ordained minister still hadn't entered my mind. I had zero experience of women at the altar other than those who ironed the linens and pol-ished the silver. But I could teach religion, maybe at a community col-lege.

A few weeks after our wedding, Tim and I moved to Washington, DC, where he would complete his internship and residency in oph-thalmology. I applied to the Virginia Theological Seminary. I was one of sixty-five incoming students. My class included nurses, lawyers, teachers, bankers, a psychologist, and a taxicab driver, each starting a second career. Only three of us were straight out of college, and only three did not aspire to ordination.

I figured the other sixty-two were like Sam. They prayed more and liked going to church more than I did. They had definitive and tran-scendent experiences of God—clear-cut, legitimate calls to ministry from a burning bush. They were nothing like me.

On the first day at seminary, I pulled into a parking space beside classmate Steve Steele, whose hair was a tangle of unruly curls. He sported a bushy beard and a cigarette dangled from his mouth. A door opened that day. Steve would go on to teach me to cuss and to ques-tion and that to follow Jesus required me to step over the line, not toe it.

My second year of seminary, I interned at St. John's Broad Creek in Ft. Washington, Maryland, just north of the Potomac River. St. John's is a small historic church where George Washington worshipped at least once. The rector (head minister), John Baldwin, supervised me.

Every priest along my journey left an imprint. John Baldwin got my attention when he pressed the bread of communion into the palms of parishioners and spoke their name. "David, the Body of Christ." I later took up the practice, which allows me to connect more with the person holding open hands before me. My facility with names made that easy at small churches, but when I moved to a church with thou-sands of names on the roll, I had to take my game up a few notches.

At St. John's I sampled a cornucopia of ministry—teaching, home visits, youth work, Sunday worship leadership, and preaching once a month. Something clicked. I was good in the pulpit and in class-rooms. I connected with young and old. Parish ministry called out my strengths.

It was like putting on Cinderella's shoe. It fit me. A woman in her nineties at St. John's told me, "I am glad I lived long enough to see you in the pulpit."

I never saw a burning bush, but a flame lit within me. I felt God using me like God used that scrappy shrub in the desert.

Yet I worried it was a passing fancy. Did I want to be ordained because most of my classmates would be? Was I following my friends or God?

My mother asked me to clean out my old bedroom. In a drawer I found the results of a career counseling test I had taken at sixteen. It did not include priesthood as a career option, but it did offer a summary of the ideal job for me. I read it as a perfect secular description of ministry. I can see myself standing in my bedroom holding those forgotten test results, my nagging fears undone. Like pulling the drawstring on a purse, the stories of my call gathered snug in one place.

My call wasn't a phase or fad. It had always been in me.

Red Rover, Red Rover, send Lisa right over.

It was also in my blood. My maternal grandfather, Harry Cobey, was a priest who served churches in Georgia, North Carolina, and Washington, DC.

My grandfather died when I was six, though I remember him being reserved and unsmiling. He wore his black clergy shirt and collar long after he retired. His wife, Tillie, was Grandmother, never Granny. When Grandmother was in her nineties, she became overheated and faint one day. I watched my mother unbutton Tillie's dress to find five layers of foundation garments beneath. Grandmother wore her hair in a tight French knot. At night she let it down, and her long white hair floated like dandelion fluff to her waist.

Harry was known for being a gentle and kind pastoral priest but not much of a preacher. White-blond and asthmatic, he was sickly much of his life. In the 1911 yearbook of the Maryland Agricultural College, Harry's senior page read, "A tall, pale brother, carrying himself as if he had swallowed a ramrod and was having trouble with the digestion thereof. He brings with him, wherever he may be, an atmosphere of pure, unspotted sanctity." To his credit he was the editor of the yearbook and must have been able to laugh at himself.

He and Tillie were engaged for five years and kept a steady correspondence while courting. I have his letters to her, which she saved in bundles tied with red ribbons. In a letter dated August 19, 1911, Harry writes to Tillie, "I have loved you since that moonlight dance at Glen Echo when you allowed me to hold you close and I bathed my face in your hair." In these letters I meet my grandparents when they were young and passionate.

Late in Harry's ministry, women began to take on leadership roles in worship and church governance. Harry did not approve. He also did not approve of women in the priesthood, which was barely hinted at in his lifetime. Harry thought a man should enter the priesthood only if he thought he had no choice—if he could not *not* do it.

My own call lacks pathos. It is more *Gilligan's Island* than *Treasure Island*. Far more interesting would be a tale where the hard-partying bad girl transforms from riotous to pious so fast it leaves skid marks. I was a nerd. I have yet to smoke my first cigarette. I was probably more like Sam Warner than I realized, but I never felt I *had* to be a priest. I *got* to be one.

No one in our family had the nerve to tell my grandmother that I was in seminary until I was halfway finished. When I visited her before graduation, she handed me articles arguing against women's ordination. She said I had her blessing, though she made clear I was an exception.

Our first child was one month old when Tillie died. Not only did Grandmother have a woman priest preach at her funeral, but a lactating one. The funeral was at St. Paul's in Hamlet, North Carolina, the tiny church where Harry last served. Our daughter, Caroline, slept through the service in her infant car seat. I remember little of what I said besides noting that Grandmother lived her life like she wrote letters—filling every line, then turning the paper sideways to write along the margins, wasting nothing.

Earlier, when the bishop chose the date of my ordination, I called my mother.

"My ordination will be June 21," I happily announced.

Quiet.

"That's your grandfather's birthday," Mom said.

Another pause.

"I consider this his blessing on you."

Harry's portrait hangs in my office at church.

Red Rover, Red Rover, send Lisa right over.

My grandfather, the Reverend Harry Speake Cobey. Portrait painted by his daughter, Elizabeth Cobey Morris.

Steve Steele and I at seminary graduation

—§—

Anne did not cut corners. She hugged the corners. She went out of her way to be attentive and caring, to add a little zip and zing in all she did, to love with a flourish and flower, to leave a room, an occasion, a friend, a child feeling special and loved. She glided into a room with the grace and refinement of a Charleston dame, and barreled into it too, with the breathless spin and spirit of a whirling dervish.

FROM THE HOMILY PREACHED AT THE FUNERAL FOR
ANNE MIDDLETON

CHAPTER 4
LOIS

When I meet someone for the first time, the same scenario usually plays out.

Say it's a cocktail or dinner party. We chat casually for several minutes—perhaps about our connection to the host, current events, the weather, our children. Most people eventually ask how I spend my day or if I have a job. The moment I say I am a priest in the Episcopal Church, I can see their faces hit the pause button. They blink, smile, and say, "Oh. Really?" But in their head they are replaying the tape of our conversation, frantically searching for an offensive remark on their part or a reason for me to think ill of them. Upon finding it, they apologize, hemming and hawing, their eyes darting for an escape hatch.

I must admit that I take sadistic pleasure in seeing this unfold. When someone says "I met Betty back in college when we were both drunk off our ass half the time" or "Bobby's coach is some sort of religious nut and won't let the team enter tournaments on Sundays," I can't help but smile, knowing exactly where the tape is going to stop rewinding. On the other hand, it is pure delight when a parishioner offers an uncensored remark—as when the eighty-five-year-old and notoriously unfiltered Kassie Minor shook my hand after church, pointed to my stylish shoes, and said, "Great sermon, and I love your fuck me pumps."

The summer before my last year in seminary, I worked at Emmanuel Episcopal Church in Alexandria, Virginia. The rector, Stan Ramsey, rarely wore a priest's black shirt and white collar. He found it put up more walls with parishioners than it broke down. His influence cast a long shadow, and my black shirts hang in the closet most days.

Lois Mawyer was Emmanuel's secretary for more than twenty years. Lois didn't preach on Sunday or mop the floors, but she did just about everything else. Barely five feet tall and shaped like Dolly Parton, she couldn't notice the days she wore mismatched shoes. She peered through cat-eye glasses and cut her bangs high on her forehead.

Lois and I hit it off right away. She was nearly thirty years older, but we spent hours, especially on the rector's day off, talking like two girls at a sleepover. We both liked to read. I got her to try Robert Ludlum novels and Scott Peck's *The Road Less Traveled*, all the rage then. She told me to read Philip Roth's *Portnoy's Complaint*. Hardly the sort of book recommendation expected from someone who works at a church. I am guilty of stereotyping too.

One day Lois shared with me a poem she wrote about the woman in Luke's gospel who anointed Jesus and washed his feet with her tears. Jesus told the woman that she would be forgiven much because of the strength of her love. Lois said she counted on that being true—she hoped that God would forgive her because she tried hard to love others. Offhandedly, she told me that she wanted that story read at her funeral.

Summer ended and I returned to class at seminary. Lois dropped dead of a heart attack at home. Her body fell against the bathroom door, and firefighters took it down to get her out. She was just fifty-two years old. I was twenty-four, and Lois's death was my first.

I was stunned when I got the phone call. Tim sat beside me, wordless, rubbing my back. I realized I did not want him to speak. I did not want to be cheered up. I was taken aback to see people going to the grocery store, walking their dogs, washing their cars. The world moved on.

I gave Lois's husband and son her poem and told them she wanted the story in Luke read at her funeral. They asked if I would read them both at the service. I was honored but my stomach knotted. I'm not prone to crying but had already shed a great many tears for Lois and didn't think I was finished. Women in the priesthood were still a relatively new concept in 1983. Not everyone was on board, and a female wannabe priest crying in her small part at a funeral would prove that women didn't belong in the clergy. *See. Women are too emotional. They can't cut it. That Saunders girl getting all choked up at the Mawyer funeral just goes to show you.* I wanted to do a professional and inspired reading of Luke 7:36–50 and Lois's poem. I asked my friends to pray for me.

The day of the funeral, I felt strong and confident. My voice got a little thick singing the opening hymn, but I recovered. I made it through the reading from Luke fine. But when I started to read Lois's poem, every bit of my resolve collapsed in a heap. My voice betrayed me with high-pitched, unintelligible sounds when I tried to talk. I clutched the lectern and gulped loudly to catch my breath between sobs. The church was packed. The loss of my composure rippled across the pews. Ladies dived into their pocketbooks for tissues. Grown men wiped tears from their cheeks with the backs of their hands.

I cried beyond what might be considered an understandable amount of time. A member of the congregation, Dan Walker, walked up to the lectern where I stood helplessly and offered me his handkerchief.

I felt like a fool and a failure. People tried to comfort me after the service. One person said it was the most real funeral he had ever attended. A kind spin on the debacle, I thought. A longtime member of Emmanuel consoled me, saying that tears are sometimes better than words.

For many years, I kept Dan's handkerchief in the pocket of my vestment. I would grab it and remember his kindness and Lois's friendship when I needed encouragement. When I rewind the tape of this story in order to tell it thirty years later, I hit the pause button in a different place. Luke 7 records Jesus saying, "Do you see this woman? I entered your house; you gave me no water for my feet, but she has bathed my feet with her tears and dried them with her hair."

No words. Only tears.

Lois Mawyer

—§—

In John's gospel, Jesus says he goes to prepare a place for us in his father's house. This is the perfect passage for Janet, who was a licensed contractor and a faithful and skilled Habitat for Humanity volunteer. She was a woman who, for her fortieth birthday, asked for a chainsaw!

Janet had a stubborn streak that served her well as she beat back cancer twice in the last fifteen years. But being stubborn didn't mean close-minded. At first Janet wasn't keen on women in the clergy, but when I arrived at Christ Church as its first female priest and eight months pregnant, Janet took one look at me and was the first parishioner to invite me and my husband to their home.

FROM THE HOMILY PREACHED AT THE FUNERAL FOR
JANET THIES

Chapter 5
Miami

Jackie Gleason and the June Taylor dancers were my first introduction to Miami. *The Jackie Gleason Show* was broadcast from Miami in the 1960s, with the opening scene shot from a boat racing up the Miami shoreline. My father loved Jackie, and I watched the show with him. Jackie ended each show saying, "Miami Beach audiences are the greatest audiences in the world!" The television program *Miami Vice* also drew my attention to the city. It showcased colorful architecture and detectives in white linen suits and designer sunglasses driving speedboats instead of squad cars. The popular show first aired in 1984, and in 1985 my husband, Tim, was selected to be a pediatric and neuro-ophthalmology fellow at the acclaimed Bascom Palmer Eye Institute at the University of Miami Medical Center. Thus Miami and I were introduced in person.

We moved from the Washington, DC, area to Miami a few weeks after my ordination as a deacon in June, 1985. In the Episcopal Church the path to priesthood involves two ordinations. The first is to be a deacon, the second to be a priest. At the time of our move, no female priests served in any Episcopal church in Florida. If I found a job, I would be the first.

I wrote a letter to the rector of every Episcopal church in the Miami area and received two invitations to interview. One was for a full-time position at St. Philip's, a thriving and good-sized parish in Coral Gables. I flew to Miami for the interviews wearing my clerical collar for the first time. Self-conscious, I assumed that people were doing a double take, as most had never seen a female priest before. At the rental car counter, the attendant asked, "What is your occupation?"

"I am a minister," I replied. I saw that she wrote down "administrator." I guess I wasn't as obvious as I had thought.

At the interview I sat at a large conference table surrounded by St. Philip's rector, George Six—or Father Six, as he was called—and St. Philip's twelve-member vestry, which is the church's elected lay leadership. I recall only two questions from that interview.

"Have you been born again?"

"Yes," I replied. "I have been born again several times. Every time I am given fresh hope or have an experience of grace, I feel that I am born again."

"Do you plan to start a family any time soon?"

"Part of me wants to tell you that we have no immediate plans to start a family," I said, "but another part of me wants to tell you that is none of your business." I saw George stifle a smile.

I also remember a comment made in the interview by a pillar of the church and its treasurer. Babe Dowlen was as lean and leathery as beef jerky with the temperament to match. She and George were in a bit of a power struggle, and Babe was a formidable adversary.

Babe said to me, "I wish you were coming to us as a doctor's wife, eager to teach Sunday school, visit shut-ins, and volunteer. I don't see why you have to be a priest."

The vestry voted nine to three to hire me. Babe cast one of the dissenting votes. She also resigned as treasurer to make her "nay" a little louder.

What I didn't know was that the rector had a penchant for challenging his congregation, and hiring me was the latest way he would accomplish that. Yet I am grateful to George. He took a risk by calling me to be his assistant. About a dozen parishioners left St. Philip's before I arrived. They could not cotton to the idea on principle. But for the most part, once folks realized that I didn't braid my armpit hair, whatever concern they had about a woman priest disappeared. The senior warden, the elected lay leader, was a UNC Tar Heel, and when he saw our shared alma mater on my résumé, he said the rest was gravy. I never heard an unkind word from the people of St. Philip's. My experience was more like Jackie Gleason's. I received enthusiastic support. (Though I was insulted when a parishioner asked if my husband wrote my sermons.)

Soon Father Six moved on to his next project—lifting the roof off the church. Literally. He wanted to raise the roof, and the money to renovate the nave. The church was topless for months. The midnight Christmas Eve service held that year sparkled under the stars.

Father Six's preoccupation gave me the opportunity to engage in all sorts of ministry. We split the preaching down the middle. I visited the sick and shut-in, and led the youth group and a young women's Bible study. St. Philip's has a K–6 school, and I conducted weekly chapel and taught the Bible to the older grades. A daily 7:00 A.M. Eucharist afforded me ample practice to celebrate the liturgy. St. Philip's was "high church" compared to other churches I had served. Incense, bell ringing, genuflecting, a lot of "crossing" oneself, and chanting portions of the service—all of it was new to me.

The music director at St. Philip's coached me, but singing is not my strong suit. One Sunday morning when nursing a cold, I opted not to chant the liturgy. After the service, a parishioner commented, "I think it was a good idea that you decided to drop the singing."

I can take a hint. I didn't sing again at St. Philip's.

(At the next church I served—Christ Church in Charlotte, North Carolina—on rare occasions I was prevailed upon to sing at high holy services. I chanted a portion of the liturgy for the last time at a Christmas Eve service fifteen years later. The congregation politely cringed as my family doubled over in muffled hysterics. Tears streamed down their faces, and those around them who didn't know they were my husband and children were horrified by their lack of decorum and respect.)

A year after being ordained a deacon in 1985, it was time for my ordination to the priesthood. As part of the process I needed the vestry of St. Philip's to recommend me. A few days before the vestry met, Babe Dowlen, the member who had voted against my hiring, visited Father Six in his office and said she wanted to make the motion for the vestry's approval. When she raised her hand, both Babe and I were born again a little. This time the vote was unanimous.

As my ordination drew near, parishioners asked what to call me. In Florida an Episcopal priest is addressed as "Father." Did I want to be called "Mother"? Hardly. In my eyes the title sets clergy on an undue pedestal, and it had clogged my call to ministry for a time.

No title seemed disrespectful to the people of St. Philip's. "Reverend Saunders"? That's not proper usage. "Reverend" is an honorific adjective and should be used only with "the," like with "Honorable" for a judge.

One kindergartner didn't understand the congregation's dilemma. "Well," he said, "we've got Father Six. She can be Father Five." Though they didn't like it much, I insisted I be called simply "Lisa" or "Mrs. Saunders."

From then on, my dad gleefully introduced me as "my daughter, the father."

As a gift at my ordination, the congregation gave me a leather prayerbook with the hymnal included and my name engraved on the front. George wrote an inscription inside with this postscript: "While the Hymnal 1982 is a part of this gift, we will not expect you to sing the service."

When George took a church in California a few years later, St. Philip's hired a woman as interim rector. Today women serve as rectors at the first three churches I served. At least four women who were parishioners while I was at St. Philip's later became priests. No one died in this story, but by the time I left Miami, the idea that a woman is less worthy than a man to serve as a priest was most assuredly laid to rest at St. Philip's.

Babe Dowlen

—§—

Mariana had a living room quality grace about her, but she made everyone feel back porch comfortable. I never visited her without being offered a sandwich, a homemade cookie, and a glass of sweet tea. She was the quintessential homemaker but not the least bit dowdy. She kept her girlish figure for more than ninety years. Her son Frank quipped that if he got out of bed to go the bathroom in the middle of the night, he would come back to find the bed made and his shoes shined.

FROM THE HOMILY PREACHED AT THE FUNERAL FOR
MARIANA KUESTER

Chapter 6
Red Wagon

All my children were born on their due dates. After the first two were so timely, my husband told his staff that he would take off the day our third child was due. They laughed at him for taking the due date so literally, but Baby No. 3 proved to be just as compliant and prompt as his sisters.

Caroline, named for my mother, was our first. She was born in 1987, soon after we moved from Miami to Charlotte. Tim began private practice, and Christ Episcopal Church hired me. I preached my first sermon on a snowy January day when Caroline was three months old. She was an easy baby who slept through the night by seven weeks. Doe-eyed and delicate, she captivated her parents. She fooled us too, because lurking inside was a loud, stubborn streak. Her tantrums began at age one. I worried I might dislocate her shoulder dragging her furious, writhing body up to her room.

Caroline was intuitive, sensing how to push my buttons or pull my heartstrings. At dinner Tim and I had a custom of holding hands while we said a blessing before we ate. One night when we took each other's hand, Caroline spread hers out to us from her high chair, clearly asking to be a part of whatever it was we were doing. She had no idea what it meant to pray, but she sensed that something special was happening and didn't want to be left out. Perhaps a desire to be included, to hold another's hand, is how all prayer begins.

Despite the tantrums, Caroline was warmhearted and enchanting. We wanted to give her everything and believed a sibling would be the greatest gift. Yet I wondered how I might love a second child as much.

Julia Gray was born two years after her sister. It took all of three seconds for me to fall in love.

The day after she was born, as recommended then for mothers after childbirth, I sat in a tub of ice water in the hospital bathroom. I expected to sit for fifteen minutes, and not having brought a book from home, I took the hospital room Bible. While I soaked I turned to Psalm 139 because I knew it had this line: "You knit me together in my mother's womb."

I had forgotten how the psalm begins. "Lord, you have searched me out and known me, you know my sitting down and my rising up."

I chuckled to myself, enjoying God's sense of humor, when a nurse rapped at the door.

"Dr. Rankin is here!" she announced with royal fanfare.

Dr. Pinkney Rankin, a parishioner at Christ Church and well-known obstetrician-gynecologist, was revered by the hospital staff. He had only recently stopped delivering babies, and he served on our church vestry. In my two years at the church, he supported and praised what he called my "pithy" preaching. His quick wit rivaled God's.

I explained my situation to the nurse through the closed door. She was unmoved and told me to get dressed.

I dried off, wrapped a robe around me, and went out to greet my guest.

Dr. Rankin asked how I was faring, then told me that the vestry had voted twelve to three to have my tubes tied. I took it as the compliment it was intended.

On my way home from the hospital, we drove by the church and saw a wide pink ribbon tied in a bow around a fat oak tree by the office entrance. Six weeks later I was back at work. Julia Gray was a terrible sleeper but happy and funny during the day.

When I was a child, my mother stayed home with me. The culture of my day proclaimed that a woman could have a family *and* a career. I could have it all. But my girls couldn't. On many days I knew—*I knew*—that I was leaving them with less than optimal care. I refused to take a week off to look for a better sitter. It would be evidence that hiring a woman priest was a mistake. I am ashamed of decisions I made in the name of being a modern woman.

Our marriage involved time management from the start. For the first ten years, Tim worked Saturdays and I worked Sundays. We didn't have twenty-four consecutive hours in a week when we both were home at the same time. Adding children to our lives required reinforcements. For two years we had a live-in nanny, but we never found Mary Poppins.

One night Tim met me in the church parking lot at seven o'clock. The girls, strapped in car seats, hair wet and wearing footed pajamas, squealed at the sight of their dad. We swapped cars and Tim, on his way home from work, took the girls home for bed. I went into the church for an evening vestry meeting. Lyonel Gilmer, also an associate priest at Christ Church, watched the handoff.

"They don't teach juggling in seminary," he said.

"It's really not that bad," I demurred. "We manage."

"Uh huh," Lyonel said, unconvinced.

"If Tim asked me to stay home, I would."

"Yeah, but would he ask?"

All through the vestry meeting, Lyonel's question loomed. No, Tim would never ask.

It also made me think of Cynthia.

Cynthia, a member of Christ Church in Charlotte, was dying of breast cancer at thirty-six. The cancer had been discovered after her first child was born. Surgery and chemotherapy appeared to cure her. She gave birth again. Then the cancer returned.

I met Cynthia in 1990, the same year she died. She looked like the actress Karen Allen, who played opposite Harrison Ford in the first *Raiders of the Lost Ark* movie, and she had the same intrepid spirit as Allen's character.

She came to me for advice, but I was hapless, pretending and praying I could help. She told me that dying puts priorities in order and that she was tired of feeling useless, of always taking, of being the person in need. We talked about ways she could give even as she was dying. Saying thank you. Telling memorable stories to her children, ages three and six. Being kind. Saying I love you. I don't know if this served her in any way. But in her desire to give, she gave something rich and meaningful to me.

When Cynthia died, our rector, Henry Parsley, who typically presided at every funeral, was at a conference in England. If her death had occurred any other week of the year, I would not have had the privilege, as daunting as it was, to be the pastor for her family.

Dick Shaffner, Cynthia's husband, radiated grief and love and taught me how tangled up the two can be. Dick was not tired of taking care of his wife, and her death brought him no relief. He would have gladly continued to tend to her every need if it meant she could live on. Decades later, after happily remarrying and becoming a stepfather to four more children, Dick told me that on the occasion of what would have been his and Cynthia's thirtieth anniversary, he closed the door to his office and wept.

Cynthia's illness took her slowly. She was in and out of the hospital. She needed help getting in and out of bed. She wanted nothing more than to breathe and to watch her children grow up and to be able to love her husband back in the way he loved her. She didn't want it all. She would have been content with just a little. Her death broke hearts and spirits.

I knew when I climbed into the pulpit to preach at Cynthia's funeral, her family and friends would be hungry—no, starving—for words of comfort. I was intimidated but drawn to the challenge. As desperate as they were to receive a good word, I was desperate to provide it.

One of the rules of good journalism is "to show, not tell." I wanted those at the funeral to experience Cynthia's spirit and trust it to be alive and whole and healed. I wanted to "show" Cynthia's inner loveliness. I wanted people to feel it and take it home with them. I wanted to feel it too, and take it home with me.

The day of Cynthia's funeral, I spent the morning with my daughters. We put the *Peter Pan* soundtrack on a turntable and danced and laughed as we sang, "You can fly, you can fly!" It was a charmed morning. Then I left for the funeral at Christ Church and the burial out of town.

A white damask pall covered Cynthia's casket as it rolled down the church aisle. Another pall hung over the congregation. Dick sat on the front pew with an arm around each child. His three-year-old son wore a one-piece short-pants sailor suit.

I look back now at what I preached and see my rookie mistakes. I spent too much time proving my theological chops. I talked about the early Christians, for Christ's sake. I barely told Cynthia's story. People shifted in the pews and stared out the window or down at their laps.

But for a moment, I did something right. I felt it. Something different fell over the church. The congregation stilled. Faces lifted up to meet mine. My words weren't remarkable but they swelled with pain and hope, and holy comfort.

A neighbor of the Shaffners told me that Cynthia used to pull the children around the block in a red wagon with wood siding. It was that moment—that image—that I offered to capture her shining beauty and how she was content with the simplest of joys.

"Cynthia loved her children with an intensity and openness that was hard to witness in the face of her illness. The impact of her life continues as we hug our own children a little tighter, reach out in love to someone in need, tell those we love how much they mean to us, or take an afternoon off to go on a picnic or to pull some carefree children around the block in a little red wagon."

Years later, people at Cynthia's service tell me that they remember the red wagon.

Before I had children, I imagined they would take pride in seeing me up front at church, leading worship or preaching.

"Look, there's my mom! Gosh, I'm so inspired! I can be and do anything I want to do one day!"

How naive. My oldest child, Caroline, wasn't the least bit impressed. "Why can't you sit in the pew with me like all the other mommies do?" she demanded. Tim had to stop bringing her into worship because she would cry silently through the service.

I had to ask myself what was wrong with this picture. A priest whose family doesn't come to church. I decided I needed to be home more. Fortunately, we were financially able to do it. I had the luxury of choice that many don't. I ratcheted back my hours. I made a pact with my family to work two Sundays a month and sit in the pew two Sundays. Remarkably, Christ Church was willing to let me work as much or as little as I wanted. For the next fifteen years I worked part time, sometimes as little as ten hours a month. What a blessing to me, and to my family, that Christ Church offered an unheard-of flexibility in the working world. Being connected to both home and work provided a respite from each.

The day of Cynthia's funeral, a day when her husband and children lost so much, I remember as a day when I had it all, a day I got it right, a day I was enough as mother, wife, and priest.

When Cynthia's children married many years later, both asked me to officiate at their wedding. I remain deeply grateful that my presence reminded them not of their mother's death, but of her life.

Her service helped me comprehend the importance and impact of a funeral. My words could matter in a way that truly helps, comforts, and gives hope. Cynthia's story inspired my own story. I packed up my office and bought a red wagon.

Cynthia Shaffner with her children in 1986

—§—

In Helen's family, the dying are asked to send back a message that all is well, and the harbinger of the news is to be a bird. On the morning after Chuck died, Helen woke up to hear a bird singing outside her window. It was loud and wouldn't quit its chirping. And for Helen, that bird reassured her that Chuck had safely made his journey to the next world. It made me think of Emily Dickinson's poem in which she writes "Hope is the thing with feathers that perches in the soul, and sings the tune without the words, and never stops at all."

FROM THE HOMILY PREACHED AT THE FUNERAL FOR
CHUCK PENTER

CHAPTER 7
MR. SNIPS'S FRIENDS

A few months into working part time at Christ Church, I received a request to conduct the most unusual funeral of my career.

Bitter cold marked Saturday, March 14, 1992, but that did not deter dozens of girls aged ten to seventeen from spending the day at a barn with their horses. They fed, curried, and saddled their beloved horses as the barn echoed with their laughter and the neighing, snorting, and clip-clopping of more than forty horses and ponies. With freezing temperatures expected overnight, many girls threw a blanket over the back of their horses before heading home.

Not long after the girls left, an electrical box in the barn shorted. Flames flickered in the wooden building. Attached to the barn full of horses was another barn filled with hay, which quickly fueled a firestorm. A neighbor across the road noticed the blazing barn. He raced to open its doors and unlatch the stalls of trapped and panicked horses. The tops of his ears burned in the heat as he struggled to move deeper into the barn. But he could not reach the stalls in the middle. Eight horses perished. Some who survived were badly burned, including Mr. Snips, a favorite old pony. The blanket on his back had caught fire.

The tragedy devastated the young riders and their families. The girls' lives revolved around the barn. They spent every afternoon there as they had the day of the fire—mucking stalls, grooming their majestic animals, riding or jumping. On many weekends they rose before dawn, hitched trailers to family cars, and drove to riding competitions all over the Southeast. The loss overwhelmed them. For most it was their first experience with death, and with the suffering of the innocent.

I read about the fire in the newspaper, unaware that I knew any of the families. About two weeks later, a parishioner at Christ Church called and asked me to conduct a funeral for the horses. Her daughter's horse had been killed. I agreed, without any idea of what I would do.

The Episcopal Book of Common Prayer covers a lot of services. It even has a companion, The Book of Occasional Services. But there was nothing to help for this occasion. Google didn't exist yet. I had to make something up.

The word *animal* comes from the Latin word *anima*, which means spirit. Anyone who spends any time with horses knows that they each possess their own personality. Many of the girls at the barn had lost their best friend.

I started with that. What would ease a young heart broken by the loss of a trusted companion? How could I honor the lives of the horses and what they gave to the girls?

The horses were buried in a mass grave in the pasture next to the charred remains of the barn. Soft, freshly turned soil covered an area the size of a basketball court. When I arrived, most of the girls were leaning under the protective arm of a parent or stood hugging one another in long embraces, their thin shoulders shaking with sobs. Everyone looked to me for how to begin.

Suddenly I felt as unprepared as I was. I put on my clerical vestments, which made me appear organized. The girls were a mess. I sensed the parents' dismay. Some likely feared I might make matters worse and some were desperate for me to make things all better. I began sweating under my cassock despite the chilly day. I had underestimated the significance of the service. While I knew I would not forget this day, I needed to pay more attention to what these girls were going to remember of it.

I asked for the names of each of the dead horses. There was Shaheen, an ex-racehorse, beautiful, feisty, and the envy of most of the girls. Bear was a sweet mare whose jaw was broken by her previous

owner. At the time of the fire a ten-year-old was attempting to reha-
bilitate her. Others destroyed in the fire were named Ernie, Avalanche,
Pud, Clover, Royal, Miss Moneypenny, and Joshua.

I invited the girls and their families to stand along the perimeter of
the grave. I doctored some formal prayers to fit the occasion and attempted an elegy for the horses. I decided not to go down the path
of offering images of horses frolicking in heavenly pastures. Respecting
what they meant to the girls seemed more fitting and uplifting.

I spoke about how the horses were ambassadors of God's beauty
and grace, how they taught the vocabulary of trust and unconditional
love without speaking a word, how they showed the girls that strength
is revealed more in control than in force, and how simple encouragement can spur us to new heights. I prayed for each horse by name. It
all took less than ten minutes.

At the funerals of a president or a high-ranking member of the mil-
itary, a riderless horse leads the procession to the grave. Those girls
stood like horseless riders at the burial site, tears streaming down their
faces, brave as soldiers.

When a new barn was built, the girls planted eight trees around it.

*Melissa Hall with her horse, Joshua, who was killed in
the fire.*

—§—

We are here today to lean—no, to bear all our weight on the promises Jesus gives us that not one lamb will be lost and that real hope and strength are possible even in the midst of our great pain and weakness. Baby Low opened chambers of his parents' hearts they didn't know they had. He revealed inner reservoirs of strength and quarries of compassion in them. He will always be a part of this family, and let us remember him for the joy he gave. He brought more love into the world, and he will shape the contour of our lives in ways that give honor to his sweet, short life.

FROM THE HOMILY PREACHED AT THE FUNERAL FOR
DAVID LOWRANCE HARRY IV

CHAPTER 8
LOCK OF HAIR

Our third child, Rob, was born in 1994 on a Sunday morning that the congregation at Christ Church sang "Come, labor on." During my first pregnancy I did not know how I would feel when the baby came. With the second I worried that I would not be able to love another child as much as the first. In my third pregnancy, I felt no anxiety. I had learned that love has no cap. I could not wait to fall headlong in love again.

My mother had filled a baby book for each of my sisters and me. As a child I liked to thumb through mine. An envelope tucked between pages held a lock of my downy blonde hair, clipped when I was a toddler. I used to carefully open the envelope and feather the soft curl through my fingers. Jesus said that God knows the number of hairs on our head. That curl made me more aware that I was a loved baby than anything else in the book. I cut each of my own children's hair too, and keep them in their baby books.

I think about the envelope of baby hair when I visit a small cemetery in Winston-Salem near where my parents live. It has about forty graves, most from the late 1800s and early 1900s. Fifteen are the graves of children. I like to read the names of the children, speak them out loud, though I am there alone. I feel I am honoring the grief of the parents by saying the child's name. I am acknowledging that this child mattered.

The death of a child used to be common. Most couples suffered the loss of at least one child. In 1850 heart disease and cancer weren't even among the top ten leading causes of death. Most people, children and adults, died of infectious diseases that we now prevent with vaccines or cure with antibiotics. Once when I grumbled about the cost of a visit to the pediatrician when my child proved to be fine, my mother said, "Never complain about paying a doctor to tell you that your child is healthy."

I visit newborns in the hospital, and 99 percent are hale and hearty. If I am lucky, I get to hold the baby and offer a blessing. I make a sign of the cross on the forehead three times as I say,

"May God the Father, who adopts us each as his child, fill you with love.

May Jesus, who took the children in his arms and blessed them, fill you with joy.

And may the Holy Spirit, who is the breath of life in us all, fill you with peace."

Then I say, "Welcome to the world, Isabel/Charlie/James!" and the whole thing gives me goose bumps and makes my day.

I have never buckled under a frightening diagnosis for one of our children or stood by helplessly while one endured painful treatments. Yet I have baptized sick babies and infants who were dead when I poured water over their heads. I don't get goose bumps then. I am cut and humbled.

Scientists tell us that every atom of carbon in our body was once inside a star. The calcium in our bones and the iron in our blood were forged in the explosions of stars millions of years ago. We are people of stardust made in the ashes of dead stars. Holding a silent, slack infant feels like holding a fallen star that was meant to shine. I will not forget cradling David Lowrance Harry IV, who died full term in his mother's womb, or the warmth of Caroline Eloise McMahan in my arms, seventeen days old, brain-dead and on life support. It is an overwhelming privilege to know that I am among the few who held or laid eyes on them.

Grief for the parents is as real, raw, and righteous as it gets. When they manage to muster hope and love to move forward, it is the stone being rolled back at Jesus's tomb again.

Hospital hallways are quiet at three in the morning. The heels of my shoes click loudly. Nurses seated at their station look up and see my white collar and black shirt. They know where I am headed without asking.

On the outside, I look the part. On the inside, I am afraid. Afraid of causing more pain. Afraid of looking foolish. Afraid of disappointing everyone, including God. Yet my feet keep walking. I remember what a Baptist minister once told me: "What inhabits you is greater than what inhibits you."

A nurse rises from behind her desk and walks with me. She knocks gently on the door before opening it. We exchange a glance. We are both in over our heads, yet we have chosen to be here.

Tearful parents greet me. Their child, born at less than twenty weeks, lies swaddled in a hospital pink and blue blanket. Too young to have developed skin, the baby is red and still. I baptize the tiny soul.

Spontaneous miscarriages occur frequently. Sometimes parents learn in advance that a baby in the womb is severely deformed, lacks the organs to survive once delivered, or is endangering the life of another. Some parents choose to end the pregnancy. Some don't. All suffer terribly. Both desire to spare the child pain.

If possible, I suggest parents cut a lock of hair to keep. It provides something real. Something to touch when there is no child to hold.

I don't believe that babies cry in heaven for their mothers. Heaven is not limited by time and space. For children who die, no matter how many years go by, it is as if they are never apart from their family's embrace.

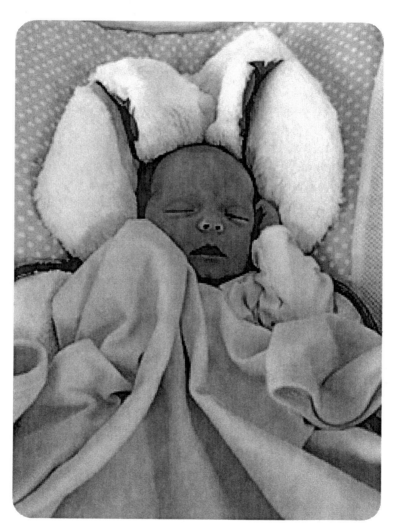

Caroline Eloise "Ousie" McMahan

—§—

When Hilda became weaker last week, her daughter said, "Mother, you can't leave me now. There are four more weeks of DANCING WITH THE STARS *left!" The two had enjoyed watching the television program together. Hilda won't be there to see who wins the competition because she has taken dancing with the stars to a whole new level.*

FROM THE HOMILY PREACHED AT THE FUNERAL FOR
HILDA FARRAR

CHAPTER 9
SAVED

I was fourteen years old and walking through the campus of Wake Forest University with my mother when a student approached us and asked, "Have you been saved?"

Without skipping a beat, my mother replied, "I was saved two thousand years ago when Jesus died on the cross."

We continued on our way. No further discussion.

My mother's response stayed with me, planting a seed and a garden of questions.

Was faith in God a ticket to heaven?

Did God draw a line in the sand at death?

What about people who led good and loving lives but didn't believe in God?

What about people who did evil things?

Was eternal life off the table for them?

My high school Young Life leaders taught that being saved meant saying, "I accept Jesus Christ as my personal savior." The actual words needed to be said. In earnest and not by rote. Jesus was a stickler about this and only those who said it got into heaven. My baptism, my fourteen years of Sunday school and church and my rudimentary prayers did not count for a hill of beans unless I said the words. My sixth-grade confirmation was perfunctory and inconsequential. Their stance toward salvation left non-Christians out in the cold. It seemed as though being saved depended more on something *I* did than something *God* did.

Yet my salvation theology took shape much earlier.

The summer when I was eleven, I fell off a diving board onto the concrete pool deck and broke my arm. A lifeguard made a splint with a magazine and tape, and my father drove me to the hospital. I was mortified to go in my bathing suit.

"Don't worry, Lisa. You'll get an x-ray and a cast. Nothing is going to hurt. I promise." Dad repeated this several times.

He was right about the x-ray, which didn't hurt. But he didn't know that the bone needed to be set. I screamed when the doctor took my arm in his two hands and twisted.

I looked up and saw my dad standing rigid, his back pressed up against the wall, his face wet with tears. I forgot my pain.

That moment in the emergency room set the bar for what it feels like to be saved.

To see myself as my father sees me. That my pain hurts him. To know deep down to my bones that I am loved.

My parents were not perfect, but when I was taught in Sunday school that God loves me as a father, that gave me comfort. Even confidence. God could be trusted. Yet this set me at odds with some believers.

A sorority sister I hardly knew came to my dorm room in distress. She sat weeping on the single bed across from mine. Her brother was gravely ill. "He is not a Christian," she explained. "I fear for his soul."

Though we were not close, she considered me a Christian who would understand her concern. I did not like the association. I did not share her sort of faith. Look at what it had done to her in her time of greatest need. Even worse, look at what she feared her God would do to her brother.

Her God was grim. Mine was generous.

The overt Christians I knew as a teenager and young adult embraced a theology that made me feel like someone standing on the sidelines when the emperor came by in his new clothes. Couldn't they see that preaching "Jesus loves me" and also warning that God is prepared to torture me in hell exposed a troubling contradiction?

Jacob Pinnolis wore a yarmulke hair-pinned atop his head every day to high school. When the debate team traveled to competitions on weekends, Jacob could not ride in cars during the Sabbath hours, turn on light switches, or take notes to help him prepare a rebuttal. Jacob was bright and funny and devout. The rules he followed were not to prove his worth to God but to live a worthwhile, God-centered life.

Likewise, I believed that all those tall orders to love enemies, turn the other cheek, give sacrificially, and bear the burdens of others were not to prove heavenly merit but to provide heaven on earth. The value, the purpose, the joy of knowing Christ is to become like him eternally *and* now. It is its own reward. Becoming like Christ is more important than any creed, but the latter often makes the former possible.

I felt like an outlier, a fake, among many Christians. And they likely agreed. I wasn't worried about who was going to burn in hell any more than I worried about a loving parent casting her child on a trash heap. I could not relate to those who preached as if we need to be saved *from* God.

The death of a man in the prime of his life laid it all on the line.

Could I take a funeral? Mrs. Link's adult son had died. I grumbled as I drove to her home. I had never heard of Mrs. Link. She was on the membership books but did not participate.

Her brick ranch home in a leafy, secluded neighborhood reeked of cigarettes. Her heavily applied foundation make-up gave the impression she was aloof and buttoned-up. Mrs. Link welcomed me graciously into her formal living room and told me a story that melted my heart.

Her ex-husband was an alcoholic. They had been divorced for several years. He lived in a nursing home suffering from alcohol-induced dementia. When their son, Sean,[1] was a teenager he butted up against his father's easily triggered rage and his addiction. Her attempts to keep peace and propriety added fuel to the fire. Sean walked out the door at nineteen. She never heard from him or about him again. He disappeared.

Until a few days earlier.

At forty, Sean was found dead in his Oakland, California, apartment. It took a week for authorities to connect him to Mrs. Link. She

---

1.   Sean and his mother's names have been changed.

had never moved from the house that Sean had walked out of. Just in case.

She showed me a photograph of Sean taken in high school. He was tall and good looking, his dark hair hanging lazily over his forehead. I bet he had girlfriends. Mrs. Link said he ran track and school was too easy for him. She held the photo for a moment. She sat still and quiet. Then she brushed her fingers lightly over his face as if combing the hair from his eyes.

I assumed she wanted his funeral to be at the church, and offered that. She insisted it be at a funeral home chapel. I sensed she felt unworthy.

About fifty family members and friends sat in the pews on sky-blue velvet cushions. Everyone knew the family's hard history. Their wordless compassion poured out.

Mrs. Link wanted a selection from Kahlil Gibran's *The Prophet* read at the funeral. It touched exactly where it hurt:

"When you are sorrowful, look again in your heart, and you shall see that in truth you are weeping for that which has been your delight."

My words at the service were brief. At the heart of my message was the proclamation of God's delight in Sean, then, now, and always. "What Sean needed to be happy and whole in life here on earth, he is given now in life eternal. The painful gaps in Sean's life are filled by God's mercy and grace."

Had Sean said the words and accepted Jesus Christ as his personal savior? Did it matter?

What good is the promise of heaven for Mrs. Link if she cannot share it with Sean?

If I could not trust Jesus to embrace this family *as they were*, then I was in the wrong line of work.

When my daughter Julia Gray was in third grade, I was searching for a parking space at the mall when she randomly announced from the back seat, "Jesus and Superman aren't the same."

"That's right, honey," I said absently, craning my neck in search of an empty space. Then she added something that made me hit the brakes.

"Superman only saves good people, but Jesus saves you whether you're good or bad."

Ah, yes. Precisely. Superheroes rescue only those worthy of saving. Jesus saves the rest of us, which ends up being all of us.

The goal of a Christian life is not to clinch a spot in heaven. That is secured. God's love for us does not run out, expire, lapse, tire, or end. We are free to reject God, yet God will not give up on us in this life or the next. I believe God wants eternal communion with all of creation, and I believe that God can accomplish what God wants.

God does not move. Just in case.

—§—

Harvey raised golden retrievers and springer spaniels. One summer he had thirty puppies. I figure that when he arrived at heaven's gate, before St. Peter could say a word of welcome, dozens of hunting dogs reached Harvey first, delighted to see their beloved master again.

FROM THE HOMILY PREACHED AT THE FUNERAL FOR HARVEY FULP

CHAPTER 10
MRS. HORKY

M y father noticed an announcement for a Blessing of the Animals in his church bulletin. Always loving to yank his young rector's chain, Dad approached him after church and said, "I see you plan to bless some sons of bitches next week."

To which the rector retorted, "Yes. So I assume we will be seeing you there."

"You save humans and animals alike, O Lord." (Psalm 36:6)

Our golden retriever Jefferson was the most intelligent and best-trained dog we ever owned. I could walk him without a leash. He died of cancer at age seven, and was our first backyard burial. Our daughter Caroline was four and grieved Jeff's death. She placed some of his favorite tennis balls on top of his ashes. It was hard to tell what Julia Gray, at two, could understand. When we sat on the ground around the hole for the ashes, she thought we were seated for a game of duck, duck, goose. Eventually the tone of the occasion and Mommy and Daddy's tears registered. On her own, she broke out singing "Michael, row the boat ashore," the most appropriate song in her preschool repertoire.

The pet cemetery in our backyard now includes not only Jefferson but Oliver, Nip, Cooper, Tigger, Elly, and Hope—our menagerie of dogs, cats, and hamsters. These animals made us better humans. They each homeschooled our family on vital subjects like responsibility, commitment, unconditional love, compassion, and joy. No one has taught me more about the meaning of adoration than my dog Millie. She always has her eyes on me and delights in being in my presence.

Will there be animals in heaven? The Bible frequently uses animal imagery when describing the kingdom of God.

"The wolf shall live with the lamb, the leopard shall lie down with the kid, the lion, the calf and the fatling together, and a little child shall lead them." (Isaiah 11:6)

I feel comfortable leaving the "animals in heaven" matter in God's hands. God appears to be enamored with animals, and certainly works through them on a regular basis his wonders to perform.

For several years we boarded our dogs at Horky's Paws Inn when we traveled out of town. Mrs. Horky was a slight woman in height and weight. Some of her guests outweighed her by fifty pounds. She always sent the dogs back home with a report card. "Elly was a perfect little lady," she would write. Or "Hope was shy at first but soon enjoyed her stay with us."

One of the services her kennel provided was pickup and delivery. Our dogs would jump into the Horky van as if they were headed to summer camp. The same driver came to get them each time, and though I knew that Mrs. Horky's son and daughter worked at the kennel, I didn't interact with other employees except the driver.

One day I was saddened and surprised to see an obituary for Mrs. Horky in the newspaper. She was seventy-nine. I checked the time and date of the funeral and decided to go. But the more I thought about it, the more it seemed that I wasn't the true mourner. Mrs. Horky's family didn't know me, as I rarely went to the kennel. But her family and staff would recognize my dogs. It didn't seem right for *them* not to be at her funeral.

I called friends who also boarded their dogs at Horky's and suggested that we bring our pets to the church and wait outside for the family to emerge after the service. About six dogs showed up, including my two.

As I looked at the steep stone stairs that led up to the front doors of St. Patrick's Roman Catholic Church, it dawned on me that it was unlikely Mrs. Horky's coffin was going to come down those stairs. I stepped inside the church and spoke to one of the funeral directors. He told me that the family would exit out a side door.

We regrouped and stationed ourselves by the appointed door. We stood sentinel on either side of the walkway, providing a colonnade of dogs. When the doors opened and the coffin emerged, Buddy, the chocolate lab, as if on cue, rose up and barked.

Mrs. Horky's family followed solemnly behind, but when they saw the dogs, they dissolved in a mix of tears, smiles, and laughter. The groomer who worked for Mrs. Horky called the dogs by name and knelt down to pet them. Mrs. Horky's family hugged us and the dogs, and thanked us.

The dogs did what they do best. They eased tension. They unleashed real emotions. They took the bite out of the loss and added a final blessing to Mrs. Horky's send-off.

Be thou comforted, little dog, Thou too in Resurrection shall have a little golden tail.

—*Martin Luther*

Friends and family of Elizabeth Horky at her funeral. I am leaning over in the red coat. Photo courtesy of Louise Bonner.

—§—

Chunk excelled at any sport, so of course he was a decathlete. When Chunk was in his eighties, SPORTS ILLUSTRATED *voted him the University of North Carolina's best all-around athlete. Maybe if Michael Jordan had made it out of the minors in his baseball career, he could have given Chunk more competition.*

Chunk's acting career added to his celebrity. He appeared in several movies, including the famous musical SOUTH PACIFIC *and* THE DEADLY MANTIS, *an infamous film about a giant praying mantis. He was cast to play opposite Elizabeth Taylor in* CAT ON A HOT TIN ROOF *but was replaced by a relatively unknown fellow by the name of Paul Newman. I don't know if Paul ever thanked Chunk for stepping aside.*

Chunk and his two sisters agreed that whoever died first would be cremated and the ashes placed in a Duke's mayonnaise jar. The ashes of whoever died second would be placed in a Hellmann's jar. Chunk died third, which is fitting for the two-time bronze medal Olympian.

FROM THE HOMILY PREACHED AT THE FUNERAL FOR
FLOYD "CHUNK" SIMMONS

CHAPTER 11
A CLOWN, A CONTORTIONIST AND OTHERS

For fifteen years I pulled the red wagon and spent more time being a mom than a priest. In 2006 Chip Edens arrived as rector at Christ Church. He was Billy Sunday, Jimmy Fallon, Mark Zuckerberg, St. Francis, and Beaver Cleaver rolled into one. I liked him right away. A few weeks into his job, we went to lunch together and Chip asked me to return to work full time and oversee pastoral care.

My oldest child had just left for college. The middle one was a few months from getting her driver's license, and the baby had just started sixth grade. I countered Chip's offer with more hours but still part-time.

"No, that's okay. We can find someone full-time to come in and do pastoral care."

My reaction surprised me. An inner voice blurted, "No one else is going to take care of MY people." Was this ego talking or God? Perhaps both.

A return to full-time work would impact everyone at home. Raising teenagers is not light housework. Julia Gray, at sixteen, was pretty certain our parenting held her back. Rob, at twelve, was small for his age, lacked confidence in the classroom, and was starting a rock band. Caroline, away at college, needed encouragement, advice, and electronic money transfers.

There are several milestones in parenting.

When a baby sleeps through the night.

When a toddler can understand a threat (if you pull the cat's tail again, you are going into time-out).

When a child reads the bedtime story to the parent.

When a parent realizes she has no idea the last time her child had a bowel movement.

When a teenager discovers that his parents are idiots.

My teenagers surprised, amazed, and enchanted me. They also wore me out. Up until puberty, children are a lot like golden retrievers—loving, playful, clumsy, and eager to please. But as teenagers, your sweet golden turns into a cat who pays no heed to anything you say, purrs one minute, pulls out its claws the next, and reluctantly tolerates your existence.

The teen years at our house were not without drama (groundings, underage drinking, car crashes, school reprimands, police encounters, curfew violations, breakups, internet fumbles, secret parties at our home, hickeys, and plenty more no doubt that haven't yet passed the statute of mama-tations). We also celebrated many joyful moments (excellent grades, homecoming court, breaking athletic records, jobs, leadership awards, volunteering, one rock guitar showman, and plenty more, but that would be just flat-out bragging, if I haven't already stepped over that line).

Teenagers toy with their parents like a rubber band. Stretched taut to the snapping point one minute, left dangling and tossed aside the next.

Did it seem like a good time to be home less often while we were deep in the throes of parenting teenagers? Hell, yeah.

I told Chip yes, and my return to full-time work brought more stress into our lives. I left Rob, the youngest, home alone too much. My attention was diverted. Working Sundays tied up weekends. My family supported and encouraged me anyway.

In my new role in pastoral care at Christ Church, I was keenly aware that my training for the position was decades old. Pastoral care involves being with people on some of the most difficult days of their life and the most confusing times of their spiritual journey. I would be expected to encourage faith and hope along the way, and to know what I was talking about. But I didn't. I had no special qualifications to guide or accompany people through illness or loss. Tenderness wasn't even in my wheelhouse. One day I wrote in my journal: "I took the cat in to be put to sleep and buried a man all before noon. I must have ice water in my veins."

I am outspoken, and more adept at dispensing barbs than balm. No personal experiences had tempered me for the job. I was forty-seven and had not experienced travail or tragedy. My own faith had not been tested. I had never experienced the death of a close friend my age or a close family member. I had never spent one night in the hospital with a sick child of my own. My husband had been inexplicably kind and loving to me for more than twenty-five years of marriage. My children were healthy and happy. My own childhood had been blissful. At the time, my parents were in good health and had been married for sixty years. I had never worried if I could pay my bills. In other words, I was completely inexperienced and totally untested to deal with troubles and heartache. I was terrified that my faith might be as thin as the communion wafers I handed out in church. I felt guilty too. Guilty that I had not suffered. Guilty for telling people to trust God when I never really, really had to. Who knew that a lucky life could be a disadvantage?

From the start I loved collaborating with my clergy colleagues and the rest of the church staff. No day at church is ever the same, so it's hard to get bored. One morning I was called upon, without notice, to bless a parishioner's recently up-fitted food truck. Dan's barbeque "squeals on wheels" and has the Lord's blessing.

It is hard to be prepared for all occasions. A typical day includes any or all of the following: staff meeting, hospital visits, leading worship, taking communion to the homebound, pre-marriage counseling, lunch with a group of widowers, sermon prep, leading a Bible study, blessing the ashes of someone's dead cat (okay, that only happened once), and meeting with a family to plan a funeral.

As the member of the clergy overseeing pastoral care, I was most likely to be at someone's bedside at a death. My tenure at Christ Church meant that I had long-standing relationships with many parishioners. I started doing a lot of funerals.

Before the funeral, however, is the dying. At first I felt out of place and awkward when visiting someone who was near death. Then I watched a hospice nurse in action. She brought a sense of calm with her. She did not shrink back, but touched and spoke to her patient without hesitation. She was neither patronizing nor aloof. What was remarkable was the air of normalcy she breathed into the room. I wanted to have that same sort of presence. I stood with families around the bed of their loved one's final hours or minutes. I realized that the more comfortable I was entering that holy tableau, the more comfort I brought. At first, I feigned it.

I did not pretend that the dying person was going to recover. Family members needed me to model fearlessness as death crept closer. I massaged the listless arms of the dying and stroked feverish foreheads. I prompted family members to say the words their tears spoke. I offered prayers as relatives encircled their loved one. I talked about the hallowed journey that leads from this life to the next.

When tiny Kitty Storrs lay dying at ninety-four in the middle of her king-sized bed, I climbed on the mattress, crawled over to her, and with my knees tucked under me, took her hand in mine. Her daughter asked if I could sing to her. I froze, then butchered a few stanzas of "Amazing Grace" and "All Things Bright and Beautiful." No one minded.

I was not family, but I became family. On the cross, Jesus looked at his mother and the disciple John and declared that they were now mother and son. That sort of soulful connection became my privilege again and again.

The beauty of the dying surprised me. Everything artificial falls away. As gaunt or bloated bodies yield to disease, they also give way to the shining within. Eyes truly are windows, and often the curtains are so drawn back in the dying that you see right through to a sacred loveliness. It shines effortlessly, like a river's current.

When I officiate at funerals I am called upon to tell the story of a person's life. Looking back, I realize that my preparation for writing funeral homilies began in college. I took a speech class at the University of North Carolina. The professor assigned three speeches, but if we received an A on a speech, we didn't have to make another one. My first speech was on organ donation. I rehearsed it for my roommate and asked if I had convinced her to be an organ donor. No, she didn't think she was that generous a person. Apparently I failed to mention that most organ donations are made *after* one dies.

For the second speech, we had to advocate a position that we disagreed with and convince our classmates to do something they *really* didn't want to do. I tried to persuade the class to vote for Jesse Helms, a staunch conservative North Carolina senator. I didn't have to make the third speech, though I hope I changed no one's vote.

JB Kelly, our student body president, was in my class. JB delivered a weekly commentary on the local radio station and asked me to help write it. We worked well together, and he invited me to be his speechwriter. I was good at weaving his ideas into something coherent, concise, and catchy.

I found the same skills coming to the fore when I gathered with family members after a death and asked them to talk about their loved one. I still wanted to be coherent and concise, but catchy wasn't my goal. Instead I wanted to capture the tone and spirit of the person's life. If I had first met the deceased when they were already in their older years, I especially wanted to hear stories from when they were young. I often asked to see photographs from earlier times.

For instance, I only knew my husband's Aunt Hilda as a senior citizen. But when I heard the story of how as a teenager she would stretch across the hood of her father's headlight-less car and hold up a flashlight for the family to find their way home after dark, I tried to include in my remarks the spirit of that game girl.

By doing many funerals, I was blessed by many lives.

There was Bud Lindquist, a lumbering, laconic man, towering at 6'4", who for much of his adulthood regularly donned a clown costume as a member of the Shriners and went by the name "The World's Tallest Midget."

Lee Williams, the mother of a deaf son, took a deaf four-year-old boy into her home so he could attend a nearby school for the hearing impaired.

Alice Clark grew up in a small Missouri town in the 1940s but was sophisticated enough to tell her future husband on their first date at the movie *Hamlet* that it was not appropriate to eat popcorn during Shakespeare.

Ruth Rightmire's husband was crushed in a workplace accident at thirty-eight. Ruth bought an old house and ran a bed and breakfast to support her two young children and aging mother. For her ninetieth birthday, Ruth's family asked if there was anything she had not experi-

enced that she really wanted to do. She requested a ride in a hot air bal-
loon.

Alex Bell built a roller coaster in his backyard, so it should not
have surprised me that his family requested that "Goodnight, Irene"
be played at his funeral. One of its verses goes,

Sometimes she sleeps in pajamas, sometimes she sleeps in a gown.

But when they're both in the laundry, Irene is the talk of the town.

We compromised with what turned out to be a delightful, and perhaps
the first, organ and harmonica duet of "Amazing Grace."

When Bishop Hunt Williams's granddaughter stood on the chancel
steps at his funeral and sang "Danny Boy" a cappella, our hearts ached
and soared at the same time.

Dot Heaslip Bard was a willowy woman who lived into her nineties.
As a young woman she was a dancer and contortionist performing in
the Latin Quarter, a famous New York City nightclub. At her funeral
I told about the time that Dot, at a church fundraiser, poured a glass
of champagne just shy of overflowing, placed it on her forehead, and
did a split and multiple other twists and turns without spilling a drop.
She ended the performance by draining the glass. Not bad for a mother of four.

I was privileged to spend time with several World War II veterans
before their deaths. Most were frail and bent over. But they straight-
ened before my eyes sharing stories as fighter pilots, tank commanders,
and liberators of concentration camps. My husband's Uncle Kenneth
treaded shark-infested waters in the Pacific for twenty-four hours after
his ship was sunk, and witnessed fellow sailors picked off by the
silent predators.

I have buried uber-talented women who were early pioneers in
male-dominated businesses. Bette Pledger, widowed at forty, became
the first woman to own a Burger King franchise, eventually building a
mini-empire of eight restaurants. And I have told the stories of countless women who poured themselves into being homemakers and giving
their children a loving upbringing.

I could never have predicted that when I said yes to Chip's offer, despite my untrained and blunt manner, I was on the brink of doing my most rewarding work.

Dot Heaslip

—§—

I must admit to being jealous of Sally's granddaughters. I wish I'd had a grandmother like her. One granddaughter said that Sally taught them good manners like passing the salt and pepper shakers together and keeping elbows off the table, but she also taught them how to burp—loudly and at will. As soon as her granddaughters arrived for a visit in Florida with their beloved Granny, Sally got right to the first order of business—a banana split at Baskin Robbins. Yes, Sally knew how to entertain.

FROM THE HOMILY PREACHED AT THE FUNERAL FOR
SALLY EVANS

CHAPTER 12
LIB AND MARY JO

Lib Gregory wore bright pink lipstick, artfully applied. Her high cheekbones and flawless skin belied her eighty years. She lived at a colorless nursing home with flecked linoleum floors and metal and vinyl furniture, but she greeted my arrival to her room with a radiant smile. In her younger years Lib sang beautifully and had a keen eye for antiques. Lucky had been the children assigned to her third-grade classroom. Lib had a history of strengthening the life around her. She still did.

"Miz Gregory!" an aide said, poking her head in the doorway. "I got some new pictures of my grands this weekend. I'll come show you before I leave."

Lib softly clapped her hands. "How lovely!"

Decades before, when Lib and her husband, Tom, had trouble having children, they chose to adopt. Tom Jr. was a bright child and the light of their lives. Every year on his birthday, Lib would tell her son, "Somewhere your birth mother is thinking about you today." Lib didn't know how right she was.

Mary Jo was nineteen when she dropped out of nursing school and moved into the Florence Crittenton Home for unwed mothers in Charlotte. The year was 1959, and she had no choice about the adoption. She held her nine-pound, twelve-ounce baby at his birth, and when he was placed in a foster home, she visited him as often as she could. At four months old, her son was adopted. She did not expect to see him again, but he was never far from her thoughts.

Mary Jo told her husband about the baby before their wedding. They went on to have three children of their own. A daughter died at twenty-two from complications with diabetes. Mary Jo had lost one child and knew that another one might still be alive. Thirty-five years after handing her baby to his foster mother, Mary Jo hired a detective. In a fortnight she had the address of her son's adoptive parents' house. On a Saturday afternoon she drove by to see where he grew up. She had no intention of stopping.

The house was on a dead-end street with shady trees and swing sets. Tom Sr. was mowing the lawn. Mary Jo pulled into the driveway to turn around, but Tom walked over to her car.

"It was like something lifted me up out of my seat," Mary Jo recalled. "I stepped out of the car and told Tom who I was. I will never forget what he said."

"Oh, my goodness, honey!" Tom's words spilled out with genuine surprise and delight. "Come in! My Lib is going to want to meet you!"

The Gregory family swelled its ranks that day. Lib was not threatened by Mary Jo. "How could I deny my son more love?" she asked, dismissing the thought out of hand.

As an adult Tom Jr. remained close to his parents, but he struggled mightily with addiction. Soon after meeting Tom Sr. and Lib, Mary Jo drove to Atlanta to see her son. They sat across from each other in a hotel room. She looked into the eyes of her baby, who was well over six feet tall. She told him about his birth, her visits to hold him, how she never stopped thinking about him. They cried. They hugged. They stayed up half the night talking.

For eight years Lib and Mary Jo loved and mothered Tom Jr. It floored the counselor at his rehab center when they showed up together with him for family therapy. Tom Jr.'s addiction eventually prevailed in his earthly life, and Lib and Mary Jo comforted one another in their grief.

A few years later, Tom Sr. died. Lib was alone. She was the only child of only children. She had no family left. Except Mary Jo. When Lib's health declined, she lived with Mary Jo's family. They called her

Miss Lovely because "How lovely!" was her standard comment. Eventually Lib's needs mounted and she moved to a nursing home.

At Lib's funeral, Mary Jo, her husband, and children sat in the front row, as well as Lib's dog, Lira, a brown and white Papillon. I didn't notice Lira in the church until I climbed into the pulpit. It warmed my heart. No creature looks more alert than a Papillon with ears extending like the antennae on the televisions of my youth.

A typo at the funeral proved to be accurate. Mary Jo chose the hymn "Rock of Ages" to be sung. The hymn was written by Augustus Toplady, but his last name was spelled "Top Lady" in the printed service bulletin.

I was absorbed by Lib and Mary Jo's story. At age ten I had told everyone at summer camp that I was adopted. I thought being orphaned made me more interesting. When I came home from camp, my mother told me that my father had not slept well the night before. He was so excited about coming to get me, she found him up before dawn, pacing and ready to go. There was nothing orphaned about my life.

I liked books about orphans though. *Anne of Green Gables. Little Orphan Annie. Pollyanna. Jane Eyre. David Copperfield.* The Bible has some good orphan stories too. The Pharaoh's daughter adopted Moses. Joseph adopted Jesus. Saint Paul writes that we have the "spirit of adoption" because we can call God our father. I felt the spirit of adoption when I met Lib and Mary Jo.

Their story preaches all by itself, but it didn't stop me from trying at Lib's funeral:

> *In John's gospel, Jesus tells us that God has one house for us all to live in together. Some of us are going to arrive at heaven with little experience or understanding of God's idea of family. Lib Gregory will feel at home right away.*

Most every time I climb into the pulpit, I preach what I need to hear and believe myself, and often it is some version of this: because God has not abandoned us, we have it within us not to abandon one another.

Tom Jr., with his birth mother, Mary Jo Tone (left), and mother, Lib Gregory

—§—

During the Korean War, Ann figured that the man she would marry was in battle, so she prayed for her future husband's safety, not even knowing his name. And luckily for Bill, he had Ann praying for him, because he was seriously injured. When they met at church after the war, Ann and Bill quickly figured out that he was the soldier she had been praying for. She wore his West Point ring until the day she died.

FROM THE HOMILY PREACHED AT THE FUNERAL FOR
ANN TROTTER

CHAPTER 13
HOLY MATRIMONY

I married the wrong person.

Everyone does. There is no Mr. or Mrs. Right. You have to learn to love the other, warts, wounds, wonders, and all, and be grateful that someone else has signed up to do the same for you. There is no one magical person out there who is the perfect ying to your yang. But there is magic when two imperfect people, not always perfect for each other, manage to draw out the best in their partner.

I married a kind, intelligent, caring, self-motivated, energetic, sweet, conscientious, and patient man. It requires patience to spend large chunks of time with me. I know the best route to every destination. I hog the remote. I make balancing a checkbook impossible. My job ties up weekends. I have a two-degree temperature comfort zone. I think I'm funnier than I am.

At our thirtieth wedding anniversary, I suggested to Tim that one of the reasons we have been married so long is because of his ability to put up with me. I expected him to laugh and disagree, but instead he said in all seriousness, "You're probably right."

For thirty-six years Tim has lived with the wrong person too. Unlike me, he is easy to love. He is more romantic, more thoughtful, more balanced, and of course, more patient. He doesn't raise his voice or curse. I have never seen him drunk. He says thank you when I cook dinner, and he means it. He is a triathlete who empties the dishwasher without being asked and does laundry. He likes it when I buy new clothes. He brings me flowers. He calls to tell me to turn on NPR when he hears a segment he knows I will like. Every morning he kisses me when he leaves so early that I'm still snug in bed. His last words each night are "I love you."

We had been married twelve years when a neighborhood teenager working on a high school assignment interviewed my husband about his career. I wasn't there, but the student's mother told me one of Tim's responses. When asked, "Where have you found your greatest success in life?" Tim, a well-respected physician with a busy practice, answered, "In my marriage."

That's magic.

In the course of my ministry, I am privy to struggling marriages. Even more so, I am privy to marriages that are magical and shining, healing and redeeming, shaping and cherishing each spouse into a stronger, more loving, braver, happier person—marriages that are making the world a better place.

I think of George and Barbara Hauptfuhrer, married fifty years. When Barbara was dying, she told me that her favorite part of the day was nightfall, when they climbed into bed and clung to one another.

I think of Margaret and Carter Siegel, two professionals with young children. On the mornings when Margaret, a pediatrician, leaves early to do hospital rounds, Carter tends to the children, fixes his wife coffee the way she likes it, scrambles an egg, tucks it inside a toasted bagel, wraps the bagel in a paper towel, draws a heart on it, and puts it in her car.

I think of Sally and Bill Van Allen, married sixty-five years, sitting at a pizza place, Bill's walker parked beside the table, drinking beers after his haircut.

I think of Steve Partridge coming home to his distraught young bride, Lois Ann, who had just been told she might not be able to have children. He wrapped her in his arms and said, "I love you; this doesn't change anything."

I think of Ann Sellers, ill in the hospital, who wanted her husband, Bob, by her side despite his Alzheimer's.

And I think of countless married men and women who bravely, tenderly, and with breaking hearts did what they promised at the beginning and loved the other until with death did they part.

Like Jim King. Jim was a big man with a big heart. A salty New Yorker, he found the South quite to his liking. He was a businessman whose success was due in large measure to the strong relationships he built with his clients. In retirement Jim and his wife, Myrtle, loved to play golf and travel. They had no children. They filled their lives with one another. On Wednesdays they held hands at a noon communion service held in the chapel at Christ Church.

Myrtle became sick with a fast-moving cancer. She died at home with Jim by her side. He told me that in the moment she died, he said aloud in the room, "That's it. It's over." He said he was not talking about Myrtle but about himself. When she died he thought his own life was over too.

I officiated at Myrtle's funeral. Afterward I made an effort to keep up with Jim, asking him to lunch a few times. He took to returning the favor. If I hadn't talked to him in a while, I would get a phone call from him.

Me: Hello.

Jim: Don't you eat lunch any more?

He liked to take me to Quail Hollow Club, where everyone knew his name. In that beautiful dining room, with its elegant place settings and attentive serving staff, Jim King, dressed in coat and tie, looked at the menu of salade niçoise, crab-stuffed avocado, and steak au poivre, and ordered a hot dog. Vintage Jim—always first class but never fussy.

At seventy-eight, it was beyond Jim's hope and imagination that he would be loved again by a beautiful woman, but that's what happened. Before Myrtle died, she had asked her good friend Wilda Williams to take care of Jim. Wilda did just that, in spades. Tears came easily to Jim after Myrtle's death, but when he told me that he and Wilda wanted to get married, his eyes welled with tears of joy.

Wilda had been on her own for twenty years after a painful divorce. She had only intended to be kind to her dear friend's widowed husband, but what started out as one sympathy dinner a week became two lives joined together in delight. Joy surprised them just when they had lowered their expectations. Officiating at their wedding will always be one of the highlights of my ministry.

Wilda wore a pale blue silk suit. Her four children and their families filled the same chapel where Jim and Myrtle used to worship, but that day he took another woman's hand.

At the reception Wilda whispered to me that she heard her ex-husband was jealous and might show up. She acted concerned, but her eyes danced like a teenager's.

The grumpy old man who didn't think he liked children suddenly had four, and grandkids too. I loved seeing Jim wrapped up in a blanket on crisp fall nights in the bleachers, cheering his grandson at high school football games.

Eventually I also buried both Jim and Wilda. They had four good years before Jim's health started failing. Wilda cared for him another two years, but she was small, and he was a strapping, broad man. After Jim died, she suffered with a bent and painful back. Taking care of Jim likely shortened her life. I asked her once if she had any regrets about getting married. "Not a one," she said. She closed her eyes and softly added, "I still remember the way he looked at me."

My parents are in their eighties. My mother's stroke on November 14, 2012, forced them to move out of their home of forty-seven years. They watched a Tar Heels basketball game on November 13 and went to bed, not realizing it would be their last night together. Mom is in the skilled care section of their retirement community in Winston-Salem, and Dad lives in an assisted living apartment.

A few years ago, Mom and I sat in her dining room at breakfast when Dad walked in. Mother beamed up at him.

"Hi, Sweet," he said and set her walker in front of her. He pulled her chair from the table, and with considerable effort, Mom raised herself to a standing position. He turned to lead her out of the dining room.

"Not until," she warned.

Dad turned back and gave her a kiss. He started out again, but my mother chided him. "You can do better than *that*." This time he took her face in his hands as he kissed her.

"Now I want to put my head on your shoulder." She leaned across the walker. He put his arm around her, and they embraced.

Change swirls all around my parents. What has not changed is the shining and steadfast soul of their marriage. They have never been more vulnerable and feeble, but what they have left between them is rich and strong and life-giving. They are discovering what it means to love someone until parted by death. It is the holiest work they have ever done.

When officiating at a wedding, I usually tear up when the bride comes down the aisle. The dewy freshness of a couple at the start of a marriage, their love and hope bared and radiant, makes me go all verklempt.

My own marriage was fun and happy in its early years, but I realize now that the sweetest and most valued fruit of a marriage ripens near its end.

When a couple draws strength merely by being in each other's presence.

When the memories and story of a marriage are life-giving and offer peace in ways nothing else can.

When two people truly become one flesh and that sacred connection makes them rich in soul, no matter how weak or poor they may be physically or mentally.

When the love between two people has indeed borne all things, believed all things, hoped all things, and even in the midst of death continues to endure all things.

My parents, Caroline and Bob Goodwin

—§—

Ouisie, who died on All Saints Day, was a tiny yet towering saint herself. In her short life she softened hearts and opened eyes to what matters most. But we would rather be oblivious and less sensitive, and her parents still holding their bright, beautiful baby girl. No good thing justifies her death, and we would deepen pain to suggest that. But goodness can surround her death.

FROM THE HOMILY PREACHED AT THE FUNERAL FOR
CAROLINE ELOISE "OUISIE" MCMAHAN

CHAPTER 14
FORD AND HENRY

Evan Ford Savage and Henry Carrington Coulter. I baptized both of these babies in the hospital and preached at both of their funerals.

Ford's father, Matt Savage, called me soon after I arrived at work. Ford's baby nurse had found him unresponsive and not breathing in his crib. Both parents rushed from their dentist offices to the hospital. In the church parking lot I ran into Chip Edens, who had been our rector at Christ Church for only three months, and the two of us headed to the hospital.

We could hear wailing as we walked toward the curtained-off room in the hospital ER. We found Ford, a beautiful, plump two-month-old, in his mother's arms—a pietà that clawed at the heart. Matt stood protectively at his wife's side, ashen and tear-stained. Ford looked perfect except for a small line of dried blood under his nose where paramedics had made an effort to revive him. Two glassy-eyed nurses looked up at us with relief.

Because Ford's death occurred at home, two police officers also stood nearby. They said we could not baptize Ford with water. His body could not be altered before an autopsy. I baptized him without water, excepting the tears of his parents.

Grace Savage, Ford's mother, looked at me. "How do other people do this? How do you bury a child and continue to live?" I had no answer.

Chip and I silently walked back to the parking lot. Chip closed the car door and folded in half. With his head on his knees, he broke into sobs. Over the previous months I had seen the energy, vision, and spirit of our new rector and my new boss. Now I saw his heart.

Grace's question stayed with me. Is there an answer? It came to me that perhaps I could ask other members of our congregation who had lost a child to sit together in a pew at Ford's funeral. They would not need to speak, but to help the Savages in their pain, they would have to relive their own. The parents did not hesitate. They came and filled two pews. At the funeral I explained their attendance.

They do not know Grace and Matt personally, but they intimately know their pain. They come here to love you, to help you to know that you are not alone and that it is possible to be comforted, to put one foot in front of another, to laugh, to live. They know, as you know, that there is no miraculous way to avoid your pain; the miracle God gives us is when we find hope and life again on the other side of our pain.

Before Henry Coulter was born, his parents knew that he had a life-threatening heart condition: hypoplastic left heart syndrome, a severe underdevelopment of the left ventricle. Surgery is the only hope. Henry had multiple procedures, surgery, and even a heart transplant. He lived in the hospital for the first eight months of his life, and after finally coming home still had forays back to the hospital. He managed to smile and laugh, and his little personality emerged and charmed all who knew him. His life hung in the balance many times, but on the day he died, it was completely unexpected. His heart stopped suddenly while at a hospital checkup. He received immediate care but could not be saved.

Henry's parents, Jane and Carrington, proved to be extraordinary in extraordinary circumstances—guarding, advocating, encouraging, protecting, and loving Henry. Jane's sister had given birth to a stillborn son, David Lowrance Harry IV, a few years earlier. When I met with Henry's parents and extended family to talk about his funeral, I met with a family who had been on a roller coaster of emotions for some time. But I was unprepared for what Jane said to begin our conversation.

"I woke up this morning thinking about how perfect Henry's life was."

What in the world was she talking about, I asked myself. Henry's life was anything but perfect!

Jane went on to say that Henry's life played out perfectly. He never knew a harsh word or faced unkindness. He was profoundly loved and loving. He was in the right hands for medical care in life and at death. Jane was not angry. She and Carrington brimmed with immense gratitude for the gift of being Henry's mother and father and for the privilege of caring for him. She said that they no longer needed to worry about Henry. Concerns for him melted away as he was raised to new life.

I understood what she meant. She was not being a Pollyanna or trying to silver line Henry's death. The original meaning of innocence is "unwounded." Though Henry had many physical wounds, he was never betrayed or rejected. His soul was unmarked by cruelty, or even discourtesy. Strangers, on the worst day of their lives, thought beyond themselves and gave Henry the greatest gift—a heart transplant. In his brief life he was the recipient of the finest humanity has to offer.

I shared Jane's words at the funeral, adding that her and Carrington's capacity to embrace their son's death with such grace was further evidence of Henry's sweet spirit and God's boundless mercy.

We so wish we could have more time with Henry and can hardly fathom that a boy who defied odds, who endured and triumphed over so much, could now be gone. By the power of Christ's resurrection, Henry is abundantly healed and whole. He is pink and untethered. He blooms and flourishes; no good thing is denied him, just as his perfect goodness was most assuredly not denied us.

Both Henry and Ford were twins. Their twin sisters survive them, and in each family, another girl was born. The boys remain babies in the hearts of their families, but they live on. They are not forgotten but remembered every day. Hearts still ache for what could have been, but are also blessed and softened by what is now.

Henry's story added a new chapter a few years later when Tommy Anderson, a nineteen-year-old member of our parish, needed a new kidney. Like baby Henry, Tommy had a heart transplant when he was an infant, and a lifetime of anti-rejection medications had damaged his kidneys. Henry's parents volunteered to be living donors. Jane proved to be a match and gave her kidney to Tommy. The transplant occurred on October 21, a day selected by the surgeon. It was the exact same date Henry had received his transplant four years earlier.

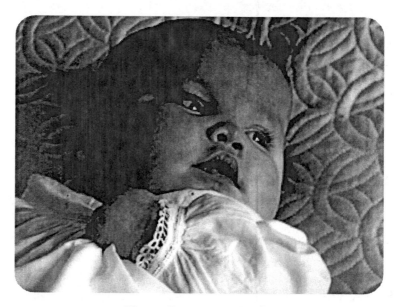

Henry Carrington Coulter

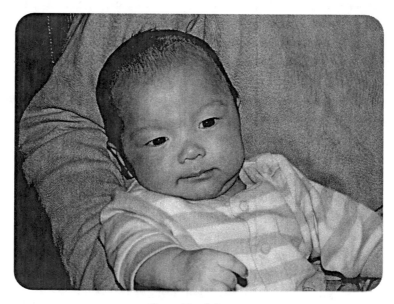

Evan Ford Savage

—§—

On Christmas mornings Clarence always saved the best for last. He and his wife had a longstanding agreement not to exchange gifts, and every year they didn't just put a dent in that agreement, they shattered it. When it looked like all the gifts had been opened, Clarence would say, "Wait a minute, what's that way behind the tree?" and then pull out yet another gift for his wife, the best one. As we gather to say goodbye, we give thanks that God has saved the best for last for him too. Clarence's life is not finished, but is just now picking up speed and strength and substance.

FROM THE HOMILY PREACHED FOR THE FUNERAL FOR
JOSEPH CLARENCE LEARY

CHAPTER 15
CHRISTMAS

The first time Santa Claus visited our oldest child, I came home from the midnight Christmas Eve service to discover that Santa had wrapped her gifts. Santa had never wrapped my gifts, but he wrapped my husband's. We all have Christmas traditions we hold dear. They bring us comfort and joy.

One of our family's traditions is eating at a Chinese restaurant on Christmas Eve. Since it is a workday for me, that resolves the dinner dilemma. When one of my children asked a friend what Chinese restaurant her family went to on Christmas Eve, I realized that they assumed everyone celebrated the same way.

Another beloved Christmas tradition at our house is Game Night. When our children became teenagers, we instituted a night when they each invited a few friends for dinner and games. The grand finale is Blowball. My Uncle Bill Cobey taught me this game. Uncle Bill, a pediatrician and a kid at heart, would wind a dishtowel around his head and call himself the Great Swami. He performed magic tricks, declaring that the Swami "sees all things, hears all things, knows all things, and tells *nothing*."

Blowball requires a big table. We use our ping-pong table. We remove the net, and the group kneels on the floor along the sides of the table so that only our heads peer over the top. With our hands behind our backs, a ping-pong ball is dropped, and by blowing furiously, we try to prevent the ball from falling off our side of the table. Silliness and hyperventilating ensue.

But for those experiencing a death at Christmastime, the decorated tree, or its glaring absence, stings and aggrieves. It's hard to ask friends to attend a funeral during the festive season.

On an episode of *M*A*S*H** a soldier was dying on the operating table. It was December 25. The surgeons tried to keep him alive until after midnight so that Christmas Day would not be the day his family remembered his death. The soldier died just before midnight. Then Dr. Hawkeye Pierce pushed the minute hand forward on the clock. His date of death would be recorded as December 26.

Lou Imbrogno died on Christmas Day. Lou, suffering from advanced Alzheimer's, had moved to Charlotte to be closer to family. I visited him a few months before he died. He looked at me blankly, unresponsive. Yet all around his room were photographs of the healthy, active Lou—waterskiing, golfing, smiling with an arm around his pretty wife. Grandchildren had made posters that were tacked to the wall.

Lou won $100 for a hole-in-one at a golf tournament. The following year the prize was a car. Lou practiced at the hole every chance he got. He took his three-year-old son and accidentally hit the little guy in the nose with a club. After a quick trip to the emergency room for a few stitches, the two were back on the course the same day. Lou won the car and that was the last year a car was the prize.

Even if Lou could no longer remember who he was and had been, his family clearly did. The dichotomy between the Lou lying in bed and the spirit of Lou shining about the room touched me. We are all so much more than our bodies.

"Hark! The Herald Angels Sing." The lyrics proclaim that Jesus is "born that we no more may die," indeed "born to give us second birth." Christmas and funerals are times of hope and of birth. We celebrate, as the angels did at Christmas, that our loved one is born to a new life.

While all my children arrived on their due date, they were reluctant to enter the world. They were pulled out, not pushed, by forceps or vacuum. I suppose a babe in the womb sees no point in exiting. Safe, warm, every need attended to—why leave? The birth process seems violent and scary, and its outcome uncertain. No baby could anticipate anything better than the world of the womb.

The experience of dying can be very similar. The process feels threatening and fearsome, and the outcome unclear. Perhaps the differences between this life and the next are as vast as those between the womb and the earth. Being born into this life and into the next involves a death to one way of being. Death begins something altogether remarkably different, unimaginable and rife with newness.

My parents live ninety miles away from me. At Thanksgiving I brought them to my home so they could be gathered with all their children, grandchildren, and their first great-grandchild, four-month-old Joyce. When I went to get Mother at her nursing home, she cried and would hardly speak. She slumped over in the car the entire trip to Charlotte. Her tears streamed as she shuffled into my house. She sat down, and we placed Joyce in her lap. Then something wonderful happened. Mother could not get enough of the child. As the day progressed, Mom got brighter. She smiled. She laughed. She talked—she did more than that—she chatted. She bloomed. By the end of the day, her mind was clearer than it had been in months.

That sort of face-to-face exchange is what God was going for at Christmas. A baby doesn't judge or intimidate or shame. Such unconditional love engenders hope and healing. It connects us with the sacred mystery that enlivens all flesh and bone. That's what Jesus's birth and Lou's death on Christmas Day have in common. Both are personal encounters with the source of all being who never stops surprising us with new life and love. Our beloved Christmas traditions, even Santa Claus, are our hope-filled efforts to create a moment of similar wonder and transcendence.

Playing Blowball

—§—

Clyde had an interest in astronomy as well as theology. The idea that his body would become one with all creation comforted him. He trusted his body to the universe and his soul to his God. Clyde chose a poem by John Updike to be read today which begins like this: "And another regrettable thing about death is the ceasing of your own brand of magic."

FROM THE HOMILY PREACHED AT THE FUNERAL FOR CLYDE ELDRIDGE

Chapter 16
Greer

The plane ride to Tennessee was only an hour long. I sat in God's lap and prayed the whole way. A few hours earlier I had learned that Greer Yorke, a nineteen-year-old member of our parish, had fallen down a precipice in the mountains at Sewanee University and was on life support in a Chattanooga hospital. I prayed for Greer. I prayed for his mother and brother. And I prayed for me. I asked God to use me, to give me the right words and take away the wrong words. I winced to think anyone might look to me for comfort.

I am very good at some things—charades, the newspaper's Word Jumble, dispensing unsolicited advice—but I am not very good at prayer. I stumble. I get embarrassed by it, especially with my family. I see too many people treat it like tossing a coin into a wishing well or ordering from a menu. People say to me in difficult situations, "I don't know what to pray for," as if God is on standby, stymied until we finally decide what we want.

Though I pray a fair amount, I am a weakling at it. But prayer improves my vision. I notice God more when I pray. Believing is seeing—seeing with God's eyes. I see others and myself with more compassion. I see God's fingerprints all around me. I am reminded why "Behold!" is used so often in the Bible.

Greer never regained consciousness. His family was at his side, and the hospital waiting room was filled with his friends. My daughter Julia Gray was a good friend of Greer's, and she and his other friends gathered at her college and other schools across the Southeast to pray for him, to lean on one another.

How could this all be happening? How could young, healthy, loving Greer suddenly be gone? How could I hold so many broken hearts at once while my own was breaking too?

When bad things happen, I sometimes foolishly think that God needs my protection. God gets blamed and is misunderstood in a tragedy. It's as if God needs a good defense lawyer to stand and say, "I object!" Suppress a motion. Bring in a surprise witness.

Here's how I make peace with tragedy. God's will is always for life. God does not decide who is sick and dies and who survives. God does not orchestrate natural disasters. God designed a world where all things, down to the atomic level, are free to give and create beauty and wholeness, but all living things and the rest of creation are also free to give and create tragedy and disease. Humans can choose to hate, rebel, and make tiny errors in judgment with cataclysmic effects. We can also choose to love, forgive, and make small gestures of kindness that improve people's lives in unexpected ways. The building blocks of all creation are free to bring us anything from hurricanes and cancer to sky-blue days and unexplained healing.

The theologian Karl Barth wrote that "to clasp the hands in prayer is an uprising against the disorder of the world." At the risk of sounding all crystals and chakras, I believe that prayer releases the energy of God's love and healing. God chooses freedom for creation. We are neither puppets nor slaves to an undisclosed destiny. We are co-creators with God. Greer epitomized, both in the way he lived and in the way he died, how our actions (and inaction), our choices, and our prayers matter.

Greer had a gift for making friends. Both boys and girls were drawn to him. Though most teenage boys don't aspire to the quality, Greer was sweet. He was genuine, so comfortable in his own skin that others felt comfortable around him. He was driven to give joy and to make people laugh. In fourth grade, Greer played the lead role in the class play *Frosty the Snowman*. He definitely had his own brand of magic. When he died, he had driven hundreds of miles to visit a good friend.

The two had ventured out to a well-known mountain perch to watch the stars.

Richard Rohr, a Franciscan priest, calls God the Great Allower. God allows us to be our worst. It is the risk of a free creation. God limits the power he could use to swoop in and avert disasters. Anything less violates our dignity and flattens our joy, for we become pawns. Of course, though theories may assuage the mind, they rarely comfort a broken heart. But trusting that God and the universe are bent *toward* you and *for* you can help.

Greer's funeral was the largest our church had ever seen. Greer had a charming and disarming personality that touched many in his circles. His friends filled buses and traveled long distances. They were too young to own dark suits. They had yet to write their first letter of condolence. They still believed in their own invincibility. They came in shock, disoriented and incredulous. They came to hold on to each other and to do the only thing they could do: show up.

On the night before Greer's funeral, a colleague and fellow priest, John Porter-Acee, led a candlelight vigil for Greer's friends. More than two hundred people gathered in the October dusk. One by one they came to the front of the church, lit their candle from the Easter Paschal flame, and spoke, sometimes with just one word, of the blessings Greer had brought them. Then, with the church lit only by their dripping tapers, they linked elbows, and John reminded them that they did not have to carry their grief all by themselves. They had each other. Behold!

I had known Greer since he was in the fourth grade. He was a good-looking boy with freckles. His wiry light brown hair, when kept long, turned into a Harpo Marx afro. He grew into a tall, lean young man. He liked having a girlfriend and readily spent hours on the phone with friends, analyzing the ups and downs of his and their love lives.

Preaching at his funeral was personal. My daughter and many children I helped raise looked to me for hope. I didn't want this experience of church to wound them further. How they absorbed this tragedy could have bearing on how they absorbed the next one, and how open they might be to trusting God again.

And then there was Greer's mother, Paula. Was it even possible to comfort her?

The church began to fill two hours before the service. I told Paula, a beautiful Tippi Hedren lookalike, about the fullness of the church. I walked her by an overflow room with two hundred and fifty people in it, and then brought her to a balcony overlooking a gymnasium-sized hall with another eight hundred friends seated to watch the service on a large screen. She took a quick intake of breath, and her knees gave way slightly. I felt the weight of my own assignment ease. Nothing I could say would mean as much to her as seeing how many loved her precious boy.

Helen Keller wrote, "Although the world is full of suffering, it is also full of the overcoming of it." The easy way would be for God to ordain all things perfect and wipe out all deficiencies and errors. It requires a mightier and greater God to embrace and overcome our brokenness.

Edwin Muir wrote a poem called "One Foot in Eden." I first heard it when a former rector of Christ Church, Henry Parsley, quoted from it in a sermon. Its message stays with me. Things happen in this life that are senseless and irredeemable here, but in paradise there is reconciliation and glorious restitution.

But famished field and blackened tree

Bear flowers in Eden never known.

Our life on earth is but a fraction of the totality of our lives.

Before Columbus sailed the ocean blue, it's said that there was a warning inscribed on the Pillars of Hercules at the Strait of Gibraltar: *"Non plus ultra,"* or "Not more beyond." Then Columbus discovered the New World, and Spain took up the motto *"Plus Ultra."* In the city of Columbus's death, a statue of a lion rips away the first word from that warning, and new coins were minted with the words "More Beyond" stamped on them.

As Christians we trust in the same currency. There is more beyond where our maps can take us here. As Paul declared, nothing can separate us from the love of God. The cross is triumphant over every no that abbreviates or denies life and goodness. So that even at the grave, we are filled with hope and faith that there is more.

I believe Greer continues to bloom in the life beyond, or I don't think I would be able to pray at all.

Greer Yorke with his mother, Paula.

—§—

During the last days of Henry's life, he wore a Superman t-shirt. Henry, of course, had no more powers than the rest of us—in fact in the last years of his life, he had fewer powers than most of us have. He required medical intervention every few days. But he did not need superpowers to lead a super life. Henry showed us that the human powers of kindness, humility, integrity, and an enduring wit are enough to elevate and adorn a life, even in the midst of loss and limitations.

We may have survived Henry, but he outlived us all.

FROM THE HOMILY PREACHED AT THE FUNERAL FOR
HENRY PHARR

CHAPTER 17
CANCER, BE NOT PROUD

My first date with Tim was a double date with Ward Woodard and his date. Years later, deep in his oncology practice, Ward shared with me that he had learned the difference between healing and curing his patients. He worked diligently to cure them, but they needed him to offer healing too. That came by remembering to ask about a grandson's batting average or whether the deer were still eating all the garden's tomatoes. Healing came from seeing a person and not a patient, from celebrating small victories and honoring well-being over healthy bodies.

Cancer nips at our heels every day. Our immune systems constantly fight off the development of cancers. Cancer starts when cells, for a variety of reasons, start dividing nonstop and, also for a variety of reasons, our immune system backs off or is overwhelmed or misses cues. The multiplying cells begin to invade and pillage healthy organs and systems. Most of the time our immune system puts the kibosh on it. Sometimes surgery, radiation, chemotherapy, and immunotherapy intervene and succeed where the immune system could not. And sometimes the cancer marches on.

When someone receives a diagnosis with poor options, maintaining hope is important. Yet if the probability of death is avoided, unique opportunities to offer solace for those left behind can be lost. For instance, when Aimee Norman's cancer advanced, I suggested she write letters to her daughters that they could read on special occasions in their life, such as their first prom, their first day of college and their wedding day. Videos also provide lasting images and messages. I have introduced this idea by saying, "When you plan an outdoor wedding, you hope the weather will be perfect, but you also reserve tents. We will continue to work toward your recovery, but we also need to reserve some tents." The "tents" are different for the one who is sick from the ones his or her family reserve. Hope is strong enough to survive healthy doses of reality.

I have not cured anyone of cancer, but I have been part of healing moments for those dying of cancer and for those who love them. Moments when the unforgiving certainty of disease, disappointment, and death are eclipsed, swallowed whole by another certainty. A wonderful confirmation of love and belonging and significance.

I experienced such a moment in Scott Cox's crowded hospital room one morning before breakfast.

Scott volunteered at Christ Church behind the scenes, quietly oiling the logistical wheels of worship. Scott beat all the priests to church on Sunday mornings and saw to multiple tasks that made the service "turnkey" for us. He also shepherded a host of sleepy, distracted teenagers serving as acolytes, and ministered to them when, not infrequently, they showed up with empty stomachs, turned white as a sheet at the altar, and keeled over faint. As my son, Rob, said, "No football, basketball, or soccer coach ever saw more athletes pass out than Mr. Cox."

Scott offered to carry the cross at countless funerals, whether or not he knew the deceased. He was also among a core group who rose early on Thursdays and slipped into a chapel pew for a seven A.M. Eucharist. After communion Scott and the others attending shared a simple breakfast and Bible study and developed a rich camaraderie. For many years Scott brought his elementary age daughter, Scottie, with him to the service before dropping her off at school.

At age sixty-three Scott was diagnosed with a lymphoma that did not respond to months of treatment. His prognosis became dire.

It was my turn to be celebrant at the Thursday morning service. On a few earlier occasions I had taken communion to Scott in the hospital. The bread and wine were important to him, like his Thursday morning friends. An idea came to me. I called his wife and got her and Scott's permission. The next morning, when I stepped into the chapel where twenty people awaited the start of the service, I suggested that we move the service to Scott's hospital room a few miles away. The group agreed with enthusiasm.

We walked into the hospital looking like participants in some sort of ancient ritual—which we were. Each person was carrying some piece of our peripatetic chapel: a Bible, candlesticks, matches, bread, wine, a chalice, a plate, table linen, a prayer book, and breakfast. Scott was sitting up, waiting. His wife and children joined us. While we set up our makeshift altar on the hospital bed tray, the room filled with heartfelt greetings, laughter, and hugs. We decided against lighting the candles for fear of setting off the fire alarm, but carried on with an abbreviated Eucharist service. We read scripture. Scott's son led us through the prayers. I blessed the bread and wine. We shared communion. We wiped tears. We felt what it meant to be one body in Christ. Even Death lined up beside us to receive the bread and wine—not as a feared foe, but as an usher to healing and hope.

Healing before death comes in different forms. An advanced cancer diagnosis often allows time for the patient and the family to say their goodbyes. But that was not the case for the family and friends of Steve Mitchener. Cancer in Steve's body disguised itself for months while he received drugs for an illness he did not have, depleting his strength.

Steve and his wife, Sally, kept a low profile while consumed with doctor and hospital visits. It was something they had to get through. The notion that Steve might not survive seemed unnecessarily dramatic—he didn't have cancer, after all. And then he did, and apparently had all along, and there was nothing that could be done.

Steve was an exceedingly kind man, trusting—nearly too trusting—and devoted to his family. He paid attention in life. He listened well and marveled at the beauty of nature. Upon learning that he was dying, friends were shocked and uncertain of how to respond. Should we call or visit? Would that sap his energy, which should be reserved for his family? And what does one say to a friend who is dying?

I remembered reading in the newspaper about a neighborhood that rallied around a man who, like Steve, was too weak to receive visitors. The neighbors formed a circle outside his house, held hands, and prayed for their friend. I spoke to Sally and Steve and asked if we could do something similar.

On a Sunday morning an email went out to Steve's friends, neighbors, and coworkers. The plan was to surround Steve and his family with love. Steve's hospital bed was next to a big picture window on the side of the house. It was a brisk, blue-sky February day, the day after Valentine's Day. Nearly one hundred people descended upon the Mitchener front lawn.

We encircled Steve and Sally's house. First we joined in the 23rd Psalm together. Our voices could be heard from every corner of his house. We walked around the house so Steve could see each person who had come to love him. Sally and their sons stood outside, hugging them one by one as they came by. Steve, with his ninety-two-year-old mother and his siblings at his side, waved from his bed, gave a thumbs-up, and blew kisses.

Always fit and trim, Steve's drastic weight loss made him nearly unrecognizable. The gossamer veil dividing this world and the next fluttered between us. We recited the Lord's Prayer and sang "Amazing Grace." Singing felt good. We improvised and sang more. "Amen," "Seek Ye First," and Steve's college alma mater fight song.

Those who came wrote notes to Steve on notecards, and the next day Sally and Steve read each one, sharing memories and laughs, and giving thanks for the fullness of their lives. Steve did not live to see another Sunday.

A few months before he died, Steve shared that he prayed the Lord's Prayer every day, but he noticed the prayer lacked something important to him—it had no expression of gratitude. When he fell ill, gratitude was his major sustaining emotion. It became his daily bread. All who joined the circle around his house feasted on the same.

A year after his death, his wife told me, "Not many get to attend their own memorial service. Steve did."

In his sonnet "Death, Be Not Proud," John Donne mocks death for thinking it is the victor. Likewise, cancer ultimately fails. Cancer strives to dominate, to survive at all costs, and ironically a cancer's moment of victory is also its own demise. It kills the body that gives it life.

Donne writes,

For those whom thou think'st thou dost overthrow

Die not.

For, as he concludes the poem,

One short sleep past, we wake eternally

And death shall be no more; Death, thou shalt die.

Most people with cancer are cured. Those who aren't can still be healed.

Gathering at Steve and Sally Mitchener's home. Photo courtesy of Carl McPhail.

—§—

On a trip to New York City, Dick wanted to take his sixteen-year-old son to a Broadway musical, so without knowing one thing about it, Dick got tickets to the hottest show in town: O CALCUTTA! *Dick was horrified when he realized that he'd brought his son to a play where everyone was nude on stage, but they managed to stay for the entire performance.*

FROM THE HOMILY PREACHED AT THE FUNERAL FOR DICK SALISBURY

CHAPTER 18
COMIC RELIEF

Indications that my family and I have grown accustomed to death over the years:

1. I made a friend at work, an undertaker who says he puts the fun in "funeral."

2. My son, Rob, took a phone message at age twelve. Beneath the name and number, he summed up the call with these words: "Dead by tomorrow."

3. Holding ashes still warm from the crematorium no longer gives me the heebie-jeebies.

Humor is a way to counter the sadness of death. When I preach at a funeral, I try to include humor when appropriate. But only once did I tell a joke, and that was at the request of the deceased.

Larry Tomlinson planned much of his funeral—the time of day, the music to play, the four salient points to cover in my homily, and a joke to tell.

A maiden aunt lived in a small town. At her funeral, the pallbearers were all women. When the family was asked about this, they said that their

aunt had told them, "The men in this town didn't take me out when I was
alive, so they sure as heck aren't going to take me out when I'm dead."

Many families want a funeral to be a celebration. From his hospital
bed, Frank Thies wrote down two directives for his funeral: "Tell Lisa
not to be maudlin and not to render me unrecognizable in her remarks." Garrison Keillor once joked that so many nice things are said
about the deceased that he hated how he would miss his own funeral
by a few days.

A year before Nona Butterworth's death I sent a questionnaire to
couples at church who had been married for more than fifty years. At
her funeral, I shared Nona's response.

> *Nona wrote about the importance of love and respect, of shared ac-*
> *tivities and encouraging each other's individual interests—and out*
> *of all those who responded to my survey, Nona was the only one who*
> *listed sex as one of the reasons for the success of her marriage.*

Then I turned to her widowed husband and gave him a thumbs up!

A few times it became my task to officiate at a funeral for someone
I did not like. I remembered what my father said he wrote in letters of
recommendation for students he didn't like: "I cannot recommend this
person enough," and "You would be lucky to get this person to work
for you," and "This person's abilities leave me speechless." So it was my
own private joke when, at the funeral of a man whom I found annoy-
ing, I said he "had a knack for standing out wherever he was, and not
just because he was tall."

Sometimes I use gimmicks to lighten the room. Claude Freeman,
a hometown boy and well-known lawyer, died suddenly of a heart attack at sixty-four. Claude always wore a bowtie, so when I started my
homily, I tied a red and yellow one around my neck, to the delight of
those in the pews. At Scott Benson's funeral, I tried a different ploy.
Scott was a good friend to many, including NFL commissioner Roger
Goodell, who read scripture at the funeral. A talented photographer,
Scott captured victorious and challenging moments for hundreds of
subjects. He had his video camera running when my son asked a classmate to go to the prom. To illustrate the breadth of his impact on others, I invited audience participation.

Apparently Scott texted on his phone with the frequency of a teenage girl. Now I want Scott's family to remain seated, but ...

If you ever received a reassuring text from Scott, would you please stand up.

If your son or daughter was ever encouraged and supported by Scott, please stand up.

If you ever downloaded a photograph that Scott took, please stand up.

If Scott ever said something personally to you that made you feel encouraged and appreciated, please stand up.

By the time I finished, everyone was on their feet, both those in the church and those in the overflow rooms, and while there weren't many dry eyes, there were a lot of broad smiles.

It is my privilege to facilitate difficult conversations about end of life preferences. In Atul Gawande's book *Being Mortal*, he offers a question to ask in these circumstances: "If time were to become short, what is most important to you?" I liked his suggestion and tried it out for the first time on a man with a brain tumor. He paused, cocked his head to one side, and as if he were a contestant on *Jeopardy*, answered, "Jesus?" Apparently, who poses the question can influence the reply.

Humor eases pain and can be the key to resolving serious concerns. I was called in to speak to John Mills, who was dying of a fast-acting cancer. John had not darkened the door of the church in years. His family wanted his ashes to be buried in our memorial garden at church. The garden is lush and serene. Stately plaques on a brick wall list the names of those whose ashes are buried there. But John said no. He felt he didn't deserve the honor. Like most of us, he had regrets in his life. He had not been a model churchman. His worst choices weighed him down.

I was recruited to convince John to agree to the church burial. I trotted out several theological arguments and cited scripture. He remained unconvinced. Then I suggested he go over to the garden and read the plaques displaying the names of the people buried there.

"Go look, and see if you are less deserving than any of them."

The engraved list of sinners did the trick. John Mills is buried in the garden with all the other beloved and forgiven reprobates of Christ Church.

Humor around the deathbed pops up on occasion, and sometimes it is provided by the person dying. One woman, eager to keep the mood upbeat for her family, demonstrated the dramatic, swooning reposes that she hoped to make with her last breath. I recall being with the family of Bill Trotter as he lay deathly ill discussing with them how no daughter had been born in his family in three generations. Suddenly the dying man lifted his head from the pillow and quipped, "But it wasn't for lack of trying."

Humor is a stabilizing ballast in my life. Those who can make me laugh from their deathbed inspire me. Finding humor in the midst of loss and things we cannot control is more miraculous than walking on water.

—§—

Jim was a tenor in our church choir. His musical taste was eclectic. He corralled his family to sing "Me and Bobby McGee" on what became his deathbed. In addition to being a singer, Jim was also a preacher. He gave the sermon regularly at the Sunday morning service at his retirement home. And take it from me, the hardest part about being a preacher is practicing what you preach. Jim had that part down pat.

Jim preached on All Saints Day. He spoke of Martin Luther King Jr.'s dream that one day black and white children would learn and grow up together in a world of opportunity and respect, and that what King hoped for did not require valiant living. Jim said King prayed for virtue that would be routine instead of heroic, as routine as breathing in and breathing out. Jim surely possessed routine virtue. He didn't have to work at it. It flowed from him.

FROM THE HOMILY PREACHED AT THE FUNERAL FOR
JIM PRESTON

CHAPTER 19
LARRY AND MARY

Larry Tomlinson was older than my father, but I could tell that he had always been a good-looking man. He was tall and athletic. His smile could shine shoes. He was a World War II veteran, a Marine in the Pacific for five years. While overseas, his girlfriend sent him a ring with the word "Always" inscribed inside. He wore that ring through the war and then for the sixty-five years of marriage that followed. Larry wanted the song "Always" to be played just before the start of his funeral. He was a sentimental guy, warm and demonstrative. I ended up burying both Larry and his wife, who he said he never saw shed a tear.

Larry was diagnosed with Parkinson's disease, and for thirteen years it steadily built a beachhead on the tough Marine until he could no longer walk and his speech was down to a whisper. But Larry persevered. He got a van that accommodated his wheelchair, and he was in and out of town. On Mondays he visited the skilled care section of his retirement community and delivered candy to residents and flashed his trademark smile.

Larry invited me to his home several times in the last years of his life to plan his funeral. He wanted to be certain that I got his story right. I enjoyed those afternoons listening to Larry talk about everything from

Okinawa to holes in one to making sure I pronounced his occupation as in*sur*ance and not *in*surance.

One day I got a phone call from Larry asking if he could come by my office. Knowing how complicated it was for him to get around, I offered to meet at his home. He insisted he come to me. A few days later his electric wheelchair whirred down the hallway. Larry shot the breeze for a bit before he told me what he'd come to say.

"My grandson is in a serious relationship with a black woman. She is a lovely person, but I wasn't raised to agree with this sort of thing. It's really bothering me, and I don't know what to do."

Though Larry was nearly ninety years old, I knew his concern about his grandson's girlfriend came from something likely embedded in him as a child.

Larry was a few years older than my parents, who were raised in the South. My paternal great-great-great grandfather Richard Henry Smith purchased sixty-six slaves in 1857 while also serving as the senior warden of Trinity Episcopal Church in Scotland Neck, North Carolina. Both of my mother's great-grandfathers were slave owners in Charles County, Maryland. The mentality that blinded a person to the inhumanity of slavery was instilled before learning the ABCs. It began with the ghastly and abominable belief that not all people are created equal and that some actually benefit from being "cared for" by others. The toxicity drips down through generations.

I grew up hearing disparaging things about African Americans, Roman Catholics, and Yankees. When my father brought home a girl from New Jersey as a date in high school, his grandmother admonished him to never again bring a Yankee under her roof. Dad always corrected me if I referred to someone as Catholic. "*Roman* Catholic," he would say. "The word 'catholic' means universal, and we are part of the catholic church, but we are not *Roman* Catholics." Dad also scorned the French because they collapsed under the Nazi invasion in days. He didn't like Sears and Roebuck because the local store would not allow the Salvation Army Christmas bucket outside its doors. He criticized overweight people, which was ironic since he was overweight for most of his life.

My parents' racism, which they learned at the knee, was far less pernicious than that of their ancestors' but nonetheless clear. I was born in 1959 as the Civil Rights Movement was underway, and the turbulent sixties was the backdrop for my childhood. When breaking news of Martin Luther King Jr.'s death interrupted my sitcom, I ran to tell my mother, who was in bed reading. Her face darkened and she said, "There'll be riots tonight." I was ten years old when I learned at the breakfast table that Robert Kennedy had been killed, and my response was to declare, "Good." My parents were shocked, but in my house I had not heard positive reviews of a Yankee Roman Catholic who supported civil rights.

My mother was the youngest of four children growing up in Albany, Georgia. Soon after her birth, her family hired a fourteen-year-old African American girl from Quincy, Florida, to live with them as a maid, cook, and nanny. Mary lived in a room that was attached to the main house by a breezeway and likely was the house's kitchen when first built nearly a century earlier. My mother adored Mary, but she was forbidden to kiss her. When taught as a toddler that it is wrong to kiss the dark skin of a cherished nanny, negative and long-lasting outcomes are inevitable.

When my mom was a preschooler, she was playing on the front porch while Mary minded her. Mom climbed through a front window into the house, and a few minutes later a neighbor walked by and saw Mary sitting on the front porch by herself. The neighbor reported her to my grandmother, and Mary was scolded harshly. It was not seemly for a black person to be seen on the front porch unless she was working. Mom felt terrible.

Mary took my mother to Daytona Beach, another place where black people were permitted only if they were working. When my mother slipped away for a moment, police approached Mary and asked her to leave. The memory rankled my mother the rest of her life. As adults Mom and Mary remained in touch, though distance meant they saw each other rarely. Mary named one of her children Caroline after my mother.

Mom had a stroke at age eighty-two. It affected her mind, and she lives in and out of reality. Mom became concerned about the treatment of the staff at the retirement center where she lived, especially those who were black. She believes her efforts produced a break room for the staff to use. She told me she survived her stroke for a new purpose—manumission. I was unfamiliar with the word and asked what she meant. She told me to look it up. I did. Manumission: the act of freeing or the state of being freed from slavery or servitude.

One day I was with my mom, and she was staring at another resident in a wheelchair. The woman is African American.

"I know her," Mom said. "I need to talk to her."

"How do you know her?" I asked.

"I did something terrible to her. I need to tell her I am sorry."

"What did you do, Mom?"

"She came to clean my house, and I accused her of stealing a ring. But I found it."

I had not heard this story before and felt certain the woman in the wheelchair was not the woman my mother believed her to be. But I pushed Mom's wheelchair over. We introduced ourselves, and my suspicions were confirmed. My mother was disappointed that it wasn't the woman she had slandered so many years ago. She had unfinished business to settle.

Lessons learned early can be slow to overcome. Bishop Desmond Tutu, a retired bishop of South Africa who grew up in apartheid, got on a plane after his retirement and noted that both pilots were black. Tutu was pleased and proud, but when the plane encountered violent turbulence, he found himself thinking, Hey, there's no white man in that cockpit. Are those blacks going to be able to make it? Tutu had not realized the extent to which apartheid had damaged his thinking and that lodged deep within him was the lesson that black people are inferior.

I never heard hate tied to either of my parents' various prejudices, nor did I hear the "n-word." But I gleaned suspicion and disdain while also learning compassion and fairness. I pocketed all sorts of faulty assumptions and poisonous concoctions to carry with me into adulthood, just as my parents had, and their parents before them. At one point in my twenties I realized to my horror and bewilderment that I harbored the notion that black parents don't love their children as much as white parents do.

I hope that what my children learn from me is nearer to God's truth than any previous generation's. I am white and privileged and more ignorant of the black experience in America than I care to admit. But I am hoping that with my eyes open to my own prejudices, I will be less likely to see the world in black and white.

So Larry's reaction to his grandson's girlfriend did not surprise me. His uncertainty about what to do did.

"You have been coming to church your whole life. You have been listening to the scriptures and heard hundreds of sermons."

Larry nodded.

"You already know the answer to your question," I prodded.

Larry slowly began to smile.

"Yeah. Yeah, I do."

He went on. "You know, I have lots of grandchildren and not one of them is named for me. If there is a child from this union, don't you just know that will be the one who gets my name?"

"And that will be because you embraced the child's mother and took a lead in showing your family how it's done," I offered.

Larry whirred back down the hallway. His African American caregiver waited in the lobby to help him home.

Larry Tomlinson

—§—

Before he became ill, Bobby's life was far from ideal, and he struggled to find peace. A stroke at fifty-five altered his life instantly in ways that seemed negative to the outside world. Yet despite his debilitating health, Bobby knew love and acceptance from the staff at his nursing home and from his family, and found the greatest peace in his life. While he had never been more dependent and more vulnerable, he was more fully his truest self in the last few years than he had ever been as an adult. We are told that God's power is made perfect in our weakness. In our frailty, God's grace is sufficient. Bobby thrived within the truth of that amazing mystery.

FROM THE HOMILY PREACHED AT THE FUNERAL FOR
ROBERT "BOBBY" WILSON

CHAPTER 20
H.

I spent one summer in a mental institution. I was a chaplain intern at St. Elizabeths Hospital in Washington, DC. (When Congress passed legislation naming the hospital, it inexplicably omitted the possessive apostrophe.) It was the same summer that John Hinckley, who had attempted to assassinate President Ronald Reagan, checked in as a patient. I never saw Hinckley. He arrived via helicopter while most patients came in police cars or ambulances. The majority of the residents were poor, without means for private psychiatric care.

St. Elizabeths was created in 1852 to care for the indigent mentally ill of the District of Columbia and eventually became a federal hospital. At its peak it served eight thousand patients on a sprawling campus with seventy separate buildings. Today St. Elizabeths has fewer than five hundred patients, and part of its vast acreage is headquarters for Homeland Security.

Chaplain interns were assigned to specific wards in specific buildings. One day I substituted in a different ward. Before HIPAA and patient privacy regulations, patient charts were kept on a shelf behind the nurse's station with the name of the patient on the spine of the chart binder, plain to see. As I walked by the station, a name caught my eye. It was the name of a college summer school roommate. I picked up the chart. She had been brought to the hospital the night before after an attempted suicide.

I went to her room, and sure enough, it was H. It had been three years since we lived together. I was surprised to see her, but not nearly as surprised as she was to see me. H. was beautiful and a gifted ballerina. I found her frightened, curled up in bed. The sounds of the suffering patients echoed eerily down her hallway. Her family members could not be contacted the night before, so police officers brought her to St. Elizabeths. The next day H. transferred to the psychiatric floor at Georgetown Hospital.

I wish I could say I visited her frequently at Georgetown and that I proved to be a steady, caring friend. I visited once. I was afraid to get involved, not knowing what she might need from me. I am embarrassed to say that the lousy parking situation at Georgetown Hospital also deterred me. After she was discharged, we never made contact again.

It was an odd coincidence that our paths crossed that day. H. spent twenty-four hours at St. Elizabeths. I held the key to her ward for one day all summer. The oddness made me feel that I was meant to have a larger role in her healing. Perhaps I was. But if God was passing me the baton, I dropped it. I spent the summer training to help those dealing with mental illness, and when presented with a friend who suffered, I chose not to help. Maybe, just maybe, it did help her some when she saw me that morning at St. Elizabeths. I saw *her*. I saw my peer, my graceful roommate and not a crazy person who had to be restrained. For me, she put a familiar face on the condition of "mental illness."

Living with a mental illness is a daily challenge, and it's largely misunderstood. I attended a seminar a few years ago held by the National Alliance for the Mentally Ill. The words "mentally ill" are in the organization's name, yet most speakers at the seminar instead used the term "brain disease." Mental illness frequently triggers excessive fear. Often it is blamed on lack of character, willpower, or desire to be well. A brain disease suggests a condition that garners more respect and compassion.

Like many modern scientific terms, mental illness is not mentioned in Scripture. However, the Bible includes ample evidence of those suffering from it. King Saul anguishes with chronic sadness and also exhibits erratic and irrational behavior (I Samuel 18:10–11). King

David, Elijah, and Jeremiah all appear clinically depressed at times (II Samuel 12:16–17, I Kings 19:4, Jeremiah 8:18), and the Psalms are filled with piteous laments (Psalm 38, 42). Even Jesus is accused of mental illness: "When his family heard about this, they went to take charge of him, for they said, 'He is out of his mind'" (Mark 3:21). And of course, many accuse Jesus of having Messianic delusions.

The church through the ages severely distorted our understanding of mental illness by insisting that suicide is a sin and that those who commit it are damned. Such injurious theology succeeds only in compounding people's pain, as well as underscoring the institution's own ignorance.

Several of the people Jesus heals present mental and/or spiritual symptoms rather than physical ones. After he heals a man named Legion, the townspeople, who ostracized and chained Legion, are stunned to find him "in his right mind" (Mark 5:15). Mary Magdalene is said to be cured of seven demons, and Biblical references to demon possession are often thought to be ancient explanations for mental illnesses. (By the way, the Bible *never* says Mary Magdalene was a prostitute. That's a bad rap she hasn't been able to shake for two thousand years. It says something that history prefers to portray Magdalene as a whore rather than mentally ill.)

Mental illness has always been a part of human history, and statistics tell us that one out of four Americans experience it in a given year. More people die from suicide in our country than homicide, and the rate of suicide among veterans is alarmingly higher than that of the general public.

I have buried several people whose mental illnesses contributed to their deaths. I have also preached at the funerals of those who committed suicide. Not all suicides are the result of chronic mental illness. Many are due to situational grief, others to crippling shame or an utter lack of hope, coupled with fear of what the future holds. But most often suicide is an act of desperation, similar to the person who plunges out the window of a burning building. Misery seems certain whether one stays or jumps. The pain of life is deemed worse than the pain of death.

I also believe that many commit suicide believing their death will be a kindness to their loved ones, relieving family and friends from the care, expense, and heartache of their disease. They woefully underestimate the devastating impact of suicide upon those left behind.

Mary Robbins DeLoache was a stunningly beautiful woman with a radiant smile. She was walking sunshine. I knew her when she was a teenager, when she looked as if she had the world by the tail. She babysat for my children. She made people feel good to be around her.

But Mary Robbins struggled mightily with depression and an unhealthy marriage. The pain of living became too much for her. At thirty-six she ended her life with a gunshot. For some people the sadness, disappointments, and challenges of life are felt more intensely. The makeup of the body and mind inhibits their ability to hope and trust and take heart.

Mary Robbins's family did not try to hide the fact of her suicide. Sometimes families prefer the cause of death to be unspoken, particularly if addiction or mental illness are a factor. But healing and help do not come from secret-keeping or denial.

We read John 14:1 at her funeral: "Do not let your hearts be troubled." Yet at the death of someone so gifted, bright, outgoing, generous, loving, and young, losing heart is all we knew to do.

The psychiatrists at St. Elizabeths told us that the mentally ill are just like us, only more so. We are all both shepherd and lost sheep at the same time, able to give help and needing it too. Never was this truth clearer than when John Lowe killed himself. His suicide shocked even some of his closest friends because John appeared to be all shepherd. He left behind a loving wife, two young daughters, two brothers and a mother, and countless friends and admirers. Fifteen hundred people came to his funeral. I had been in communication with John in the weeks before his death. I, along with a few others, was very aware of his depression and sought to get him help. I asked John if he had considered suicide. He said no.

Preaching at his funeral was daunting. I knew three generations of his family. I struggled with my own sense of having failed John. The family gave me permission to speak about the elephant in the room, to talk about his depression and to use the words "mental illness." I remembered what a widow had said to me a few months earlier and used her analogy in my homily.

Some of us limp on the outside—our challenge noticeable to all. And some of us limp on the inside, and the struggle is invisible. Mental illness can cripple. It can be a malignancy that erodes hope and distorts reality.

For those trapped in depression the thinking frequently goes like this: "I am hurting people. I'm unhappy and making others unhappy. I can't fix my life. It would be better for everyone if I were gone, if no one had to worry about me anymore." That's the backward logic that is at work. John was the sort of person who always thought of others before himself. Though it makes no sense to us, I believe John did what he did out of love and concern for everyone but himself.

Speaking about mental illness was the easy part. It was talking about God that stymied me. Saying that God would heal our broken hearts seemed disingenuous and empty. God had not healed John. Why should God be trusted now?

The night before John's funeral, I went to bed with my homily unfinished. I rose early the next morning, looking for words about God I could say with integrity. I felt distant and let down. Why wasn't God helping me help all the grief-stricken people who were gathering in a few short hours? I also felt silly. What burdened me was child's play next to what John's family carried.

John's burial in our church's memorial garden was at 10:00 A.M., for the family only. The funeral was later in the afternoon. Chip Edens, the rector of Christ Church, and I headed to the garden about fifteen minutes before the family was to arrive. We were taken aback to see one of our preschool teachers in the garden with her class of three-year-old children, all of whom were squealing with delight and excitement.

What is she doing? I thought with irritation. She knows we have a funeral today. The freshly dug hole for the ashes is right behind her. She needs to get those kids out of here before the family shows up.

Chip and I hurried over to the teacher and children, annoyance written across my face. The teacher, Missy Hill, was holding a collapsible mesh bag. "We're releasing the butterflies we raised this spring," she explained, looking up at us and smiling as an orange butterfly fluttered up into the air between us. The children cheered and clapped.

I fell back on my heels as three more butterflies took wing.

Release. That was it. I felt God reaching out to me. Is this why I couldn't finish my homily? Because here is where I would find the words? After the burial in the garden, I wept alone in the clergy vesting room. Then I went back to my office and finished my homily.

Jesus's own life and death are witness to the fact that not all things can be fixed or cured, no matter how hard you try or how good you are. The resurrection, however, reveals that all things can be redeemed, healed, and made new. Death does not have the last word, for us or for John. The peace and healing that eluded him here, he is now free to receive and trust. He is perfectly unburdened.

God reminded me of his presence and power to resurrect this morning.

I went on to tell the congregation about the butterflies, and offered the words that they had given to me.

Four butterflies flew out and around the garden just moments before we laid John's ashes to rest. The butterflies were not the only ones released. Ultimately I trust that God, who filled John with so much genuine goodness, can be trusted to release John and us, and provide us wings of hope and healing.

The response I received after John's funeral was the largest I have ever known. I was not the only one who needed to be released. People were grateful that John's family had allowed me to be honest about his illness. Some told me of suicides in their own families. One man decided to stop hiding his own struggle and started telling friends about his depression. Many took the time to write me a note, or text or email me their appreciation.

One letter blew me away. It was written by someone I didn't know. She said that her son had committed suicide twelve years ago, at age forty-one. She wrote: "What you said at John's service was more comforting to me than anything I have experienced since my son's death."

Her letter is the single most meaningful letter I have received in my ministry. It overwhelms me to think that my words could bring the first real comfort to a mother who had been grieving the suicide of her son for twelve years. If that were the only thing I accomplished in my thirty-plus years of ministry, it would be enough.

Mental illness is often highly treatable, but its stigma makes it hard for people to ask for, pay for, pray for, and hope for help. Our natural reaction can be to take a step backward when we learn that someone has a brain disease, as I did with H. when I saw her curled up in bed. I don't know what became of H., but I know what she, and others who suffered like her, changed in me. A step toward someone, instead of away, will bring all of us nearer to a change of heart and mind.

Mary Robbins DeLoache

—§—

John flew twenty-six missions during World War II in a P51 Mustang single-seat fighter plane, escorting bombers on raids into Germany. Much later in life John was invited back into the cockpit of a refurbished P51 training plane. Unlike the actual Mustang, the training plane had no canopy and looked just a few versions better than the one at Kitty Hawk. At eighty-six years old, John grabbed that throttle and with his white hair blowing in the wind, flew the skies again. He even took the plane into a loop while his son watched in horror and amazement from the ground below.

FROM THE HOMILY PREACHED AT THE FUNERAL FOR
JOHN MCALISTER

CHAPTER 21
MORE THAN LUCK

I have found a quick way to feel twenty years younger. It doesn't involve surgery, a cream, Spandex, or drugs. I spend time at a retirement community and I feel hip, fashionable, and fleet of foot.

I joined my parents for bingo at the retirement community where they live. The bingo cards were the type with miniature sliding doors over each number. I picked up three cards out of the bin for myself, figuring I could easily keep up. An octogenarian resident served as the bingo caller, and she meant business. She alerted me to the "two-card maximum" rule. Before the game began, my dad smacked the edge of his card on the table to knock all the little sliding doors open. Over the microphone, the bingo tsarina immediately scolded, "Do *not* bang the cards on the table." For my dad, that was like saying sic 'em to a dog. Not only did he enjoy breaking rules, but with his short-term memory issues he couldn't remember them. He banged his card all night, much to her consternation. If they were younger or more mobile, they might have come to blows.

Before the first number, I leaned back in my chair, counting on a relaxing parlor game. Within fifteen seconds I was sitting up, smartly at attention, scanning my cards. This was not your grandma's bingo. The tsarina must have had a background in auctioneering. She was calling out numbers in rapid-fire clip. Most folks knew the drill, and were on point, but others lagged behind.

"I can't hear what she's saying, can you?"

"Is that a six or an eight on my card?"

"Have we started yet?"

Winners got to make a trip to the prize table. When my mother won, I rolled her over to the table to select her prize. Bags of assorted candies were available, but most of the prizes seemed to come from Walgreens. Toothpaste, a bottle of Windex, soap, Saran Wrap, wax paper, bobby pins—and I am not making this up—a box of Kotex.

Bingo is a game of luck, and luck is involved in aging too. Even the fittest among us can wind up disabled or suffering dementia.

Comedian George Carlin had a great idea:

I want to live my next life backwards:

You start out dead and get that out of the way.

Then you wake up in a nursing home feeling better every day.

Then you get kicked out for being too healthy.

You enjoy your retirement and collect your pension.

Then when you start work, you get a gold watch on your first day.

You work forty years until you're too young to work.

You get ready for high school: drink alcohol, party.

Then you go to primary school, you become a kid, you play, and you have no responsibilities.

Then you become a baby, and then ...

You spend your last nine months floating peacefully in luxury, in spa-like conditions: central heating, room service on tap, and then ...

You finish off with an orgasm. I rest my case.

One of my many mentors on aging well was Muriel Livingston. Although she was forty-five years older, Muriel and I were friends. When she became housebound, we grew closer. Muriel was witty and well traveled. A former librarian and French teacher, she possessed a wonderful way with words. Near the end of her life, past ninety and no longer walking, she stunned me when she introduced me to someone and also told her the names of all my children. I regret that I didn't bring any of them to meet her.

Since she could not get to church, Muriel and I shared communion at her home. As I closed our time with prayer, Muriel squeezed my hand and gently prayed aloud for strength and offered thanks for me. A visit with Muriel was an anointing.

It had been decades since I had cried at Lois Mawyer's funeral. I had teared up at funerals or cried afterward, but I had never broken down again until Muriel's service. My reaction caught me by surprise. I began crying while saying these words, and the tears flowed nonstop for the remainder of the service.

When Muriel befriended people of all generations, she taught me that age is not a barrier to being a friend. When she took a leadership role in the Irish Children's Program, she taught me that someone in her seventies who weighs 110 pounds can make a difference for peace in this world. When Muriel established a library at Christ Church, she taught me that a good idea, a willingness to serve, and a commitment to excellence can create something from nothing. When at nearly ninety she lost her son, she taught me that a mother never stops loving her children with her whole heart. When she preferred to talk about global events instead of her own aches and slow decline, she taught me that even when one's body and world is shrinking, one's mind and heart do not have to. When she broke a bone and spent weeks in rehab at a nursing home and recovered, she taught me about resilience and hope. When she spoke of her great-grandchildren, all of whom she declared to be brilliant and beautiful, she taught me that there is joy in all stages of life.

I think of Muriel often, even when I am doing laundry. Muriel hung her college diploma in the laundry room to remind herself while doing housework that she was an educated woman. My college diploma now hangs over my washing machine.

Here are some of the things I have learned from Muriel, and others, about aging with guts and grace.

1. If I make it into my nineties unscathed, most of my friends will be dead or demented. I'll need to make younger friends, involve myself in things younger people do. A sport, hammering for Habitat, joining a book club, volunteering at a school or church or for a nonprofit or political campaign. If I want younger friends, I can't talk all the time. I have to listen. Ask questions. Complaining pushes people away. Making people feel good draws them closer.

   Everyone likes to feel blessed. In his day, the apostle Peter became so popular that people brought the sick into the streets "so that at least Peter's shadow might fall on some of them as he passed by" (Acts 5:15). I will not make friends by being critical and negative. I want to bless those on whom my shadow falls.

2. Maintain or develop an interest that my hands will remember how to do when my brain no longer can. For instance, playing a musical instrument, knitting, needlework, woodworking, or painting. My hands will probably always remember how to type even if all I write is gibberish. "asdfjkl;" isn't going anywhere.

   The gaming center of the brain retains memory well. People can play Scrabble, bridge, or pinochle even when they can't remember what day or year it is. My dad beats me regularly at gin rummy, yet he keeps asking the whereabouts of his car, which has been gone for months. I bet when my son and his friends move into nursing homes, they will play video games as competently as they do now. Their fingers will remember how to get to the next level.

   When Bill Nichols Sr. stopped smoking, he needed to keep his hands busy. Bill was well over six feet, a Marine who served in World War II. His wife suggested needlepoint. At his funeral I carried into the pulpit a brick doorstop cover he had needlepointed, stitching my name on one side. I also held up a Christmas pillow that Bill made for me with the holy family on the front. Bill completed one of the needlepointed kneeling cushions at our altar. He made enormous Christmas stockings for each of his grandchildren. His needlepoint stemmed from a combination of his thoughtfulness and his faithfulness. I don't know that I have had anyone devote as much time to a gift for me as Bill did.

3. If I am lucky enough to have grandchildren, I will do more than love them from a distance. If grandchildren aren't in the cards, there are plenty of other children to "adopt." In *The Road to Character*, David Brooks talks about the difference between résumé virtues and eulogy virtues. The way we want to be remembered in a eulogy is likely very different from what we would put on a résumé. I am moved when a grandchild speaks at a funeral with heartfelt affection about a grandparent. It is an expectation to impact your child's life in a positive way, even an obligation. But to impact a grandchild in an enduring, life-giving way is a gift, a privilege, a joy, and one of the signs of a blessed and well-prioritized life.

    I want the chance to cultivate a relationship with at least one grandchild, to make a grandchild feel she is perfectly enough, to love him in a way that he will draw strength from the rest of his life. Wouldn't that be grand?

    Jack Reeves was dying, and what was on his bucket list? To be able to hold all three of his great-grandchildren at the same time. He checked that off a few weeks before he died. Bill Baynard used to tell his grandchildren about a hidden treasure. They hung on his every word. "The treasure can be found over the ... right next to ..." Then Bill would pretend to fall asleep, snoring loudly, never disclosing the treasure's whereabouts. Bill's family finally learned exactly where the storied treasure was hidden. As I said at his funeral, the treasure was Bill himself. Not hidden but in plain sight. Being loved by him was precious and invaluable, and a fortune that is theirs forever.

4. Stay engaged. Isolation shrinks a life. Remain reasonably current with technology. My generation never imagined a day when the postal service and a telephone that plugs into the wall would go the way of the Pony Express and smoke signals. Who knows what devices and technologies are coming down the pike? I don't want to forget how maddening it was to teach my parents how to use a cell phone. (A friend's father would turn on his phone to

make a call and otherwise kept it off, while another friend's ninety-three-year-old father wields his iPhone as deftly as a teenager.)

Staying engaged means being able to follow what's going on around me. I got hearing aids when my family kept telling me I was going deaf. I realized that being able to distinguish between my daughter saying "I got some cute tops" from "I got some tube tops" is nice, but what's more important is keeping in the loop, in the flow of conversation. If I make people repeat themselves, eventually they will avoid talking to me.

5. Die early and often. Bury resentments and grudges. Stop giving CPR to regrets. Pull the plug on pettiness and that nasty need to be right. Jesus teaches that death is the path to resurrection and transformation, but death is not just for the dying. Those of us alive and kicking can stand to experience a little death too. Following Jesus involves dying a string of little deaths in this life, but it also means being raised up by a pearl strand of glorious resurrections.

Adelaide Ingle knew more than just little deaths in her life. Her husband had a stroke and was bedridden for more than a decade. An accident disabled her son. Two of her grandchildren died, one in a fire and the other in a car crash. But as I said at her funeral, Adelaide chose along the way to grow, to embrace, to love, to forgive, and to give. That's what kept her young, made her wise, and made her loving and loveable. That's what made her shine brightly well into her nineties and made people want to be near her.

Growing older means that eventually the funeral will be my own. We are fortunate to live in a time when modern medicine gives people longer and healthier lives. After being relatively stagnant for two millennia, the average life expectancy doubled over the last hundred and fifty years, from forty to eighty years of age. Childhood mortality rates plummeted with the onset of vaccinations and antibiotics. The rate of women dying in childbirth dropped over 97 percent in the last century. Medication and surgical procedures have drastically lowered deaths from heart disease.

The book *Modern Death* by Haider Warraich reports how scientific advances affect how people die. In 1960 only 1 percent of Americans were admitted to the hospital in the last year of their life. By 1987 50 percent were hospitalized for at least one night. Today 20 percent of Americans undergo a surgical procedure in the last month of life. Longer lives mean many live beyond the vigor of their brains or bodies. We experience a new phenomenon that is being called the survival of the unfittest.

People say to me, "I just want to wake up dead one day." Dying with our boots on means dying while we are still active, sane, and spending our days doing what we love. Such deaths happen every day, but the loved ones left behind struggle with the suddenness of their loss and feel that they and the deceased have been robbed. Those whose loved ones die after extended illnesses also grieve deeply but can often see how the future primarily held further painful decline and loss of dignity.

Dementia runs in my family. I shudder to think what I might put my children and husband through. If I am to die before I reach eighty, I would prefer to die of an illness where I know of my impending death in advance. I would like time to say or do anything left undone, to leave letters for my grandchildren, to give away possessions that are meaningful to me and might be meaningful for others, to eat all the ice cream I want, and to thank the people who care for me. But after eighty, even if I am still as healthy as a horse and have all my marbles, I would be content to wake up dead one day. Sign me up for dying on a trip to Italy or after a week at the beach with my family.

People often say that life is short. Sometimes it is, but death always is. "Today I will see you in paradise," Jesus told the thief hanging on the cross next to him. Today. Not some distant judgment day. Death is but a moment. Our hearts quit beating. Our amazing body runs out of steam, whether after a long run or before we barely get started. But death is quickly overcome by the dogged, indomitable, divine force of life within the core of each of us. Death is short. We enjoy spectacular glimmers now, but life on the other side promises to be singularly exquisite.

Muriel Livingston

—§—

Helen loved lighthouses and at one point she and her family were on a mission to visit as many lighthouses as they could. On a table in their home are miniatures of all the lighthouses they visited. The thing about lighthouses—they don't shoot off cannons or fireworks; they just shine, steadily and quietly. Helen was a lot like the lighthouses she collected.

FROM THE HOMILY PREACHED AT THE FUNERAL FOR
HELEN SAUNDERS MYERS

CHAPTER 22
PANEGYRIC

A few years ago I stood with my two sisters on the front stoop of the Giles Apartment building in Richmond, Virginia, where our father spent the first five years of his life. A sign on the front lawn advertised one- and two-bedroom units for rent. Curling black-and-white photos show our father standing in the same spot. In one, he is with his parents. In another, he wears a policeman costume.

The apartment was one block from Monument Avenue's Stuart Circle and directly across the street from St. James Episcopal Church, a block away from a United Church of Christ parish. My grandparents did not go to church, but each week they sent their son to the Episcopalians. In Dad's baby book is a picture of him in front of St. James and a certificate of his completion of three-year-old church school. In my grandmother's handwriting, she notes that he received an award for perfect attendance.

Dad later met my mother at an Episcopal church. Mom's father, Harry, was the visiting preacher at St. Paul's Episcopal Church in Winston-Salem in the summer of 1948. Dad was the head acolyte at St. Paul's and was asked to entertain the guest minister's children. Mom was seventeen. Dad was eighteen. He went a little overboard in his charge.

While I might think my call to ministry began within my own life-time, part of why I am an Episcopal priest today—in fact, why I *am* at all—is because the Giles Apartments were closer to St. James Episcopal Church than the UCC church one block to the east.

I hardly knew my paternal grandparents. I am told that I favor my grandmother Lillian in temperament. She did everything quickly, a trait of mine as well. She wrote clever poetry, and while I am not a poet, I like fine rhyme. Her husband, my grandfather, was the chief financial officer of Wachovia Bank, but feisty Grandmother Lillian re-fused to bank at Wachovia because she didn't like how they treated her husband.

I stood on the block where my young and vibrant grandmother once strolled her baby and where each week she walked him across the street for church school. Her life pushes through time and generations, holding hands with mine. The apartment building still stands, just as my grandparents still profoundly affect my life.

Death does not diminish, stall, or hinder love. In the letter to the Hebrews, Paul talks about those who have gone before, saying that a cloud of witnesses surround us. We are not just surrounded. They live on within us and beyond us. Not as wispy ghosts, but fully alive, made new, made whole.

I attended a funeral in which the family members' remarks were listed in the program as the "panegyric." The word was new to me. A panegyric is a speech given in praise of someone, like a eulogy. Turns out I am a professional panegyrist.

People ask me if I find it depressing to officiate at funerals. Certain-ly it is hard to say goodbye to those I love and admire, but most of the time I find it to be a blessed honor and privilege, for two reasons. First, I have the hope of the resurrection to proclaim. As Frederick Buechner wrote, "The resurrection means that the worst thing is never the last thing." By the mercies of God, healing and wholeness prevail. And sec-ond, it is uplifting and precious to witness the loving legacy of a life. I am a repository of hundreds of sacred stories.

Jim Butterworth planned his service two years before he died. He prepaid the funeral home and became the first person at our church to pay in advance for the brass plate that goes on the wall of the gar-den where his ashes are buried. Handsome, long-legged, and lean, it wasn't hard to believe that he had dug his oars into the water for the

1952 rowing squad at Princeton. His blue eyes were hooded with long lashes, and his deep voice was honeyed and mellifluous. Jim and his wife, Nona, sang all their life, often members of more than one choir at a time.

I visited Jim ten days before he died. He knew he was dying, and he reminded me that he hoped a selection from Bach's *St. Matthew Passion* could be played at his service. He sang a few bars of it in his lovely bass voice. He first sang the *Passion* when he was a member of the Orpheus Club, an all-male singing group in Philadelphia that still exists today. Jim recounted how they sang in tux and tails, and during intermission dropped by a bar across the street to wet their dry throats. When the group sang musicals, some dressed as women for the female parts. Jim said that in a wig, he looked just like his mother. When the Orpheus Club sang the *Passion*, Jim remembered that the beauty and power of the music overwhelmed the choir and full orchestra. The violin section played with tears streaming down their faces. Fifty years past, on his deathbed, Jim's long eyelashes were wet with tears as he told the story.

Days later, I sat around the kitchen table with Jim's children and watched them unpack a treasure trove of memories with their dad. They doubled over laughing in the retelling of some stories, and in others, tears flowed as had Jim's. Jim died, but he was hardly gone. No doubt he lives on in his children and grandchildren, and in me. One day a great-great-grandchild of his will hear Bach's *Passion* for the first time. The hands of the clock will swiftly twirl back, folding generations, and a glorious chorus including Bach, Jim, Nona, and a weeping violinist will leave another set of long-lashed, blue eyes pooled with inexplicable tears.

My greatest panegyric is for the God whose generosity and insistent love makes that possible. Death appears to be desertion. Both the dying and the bereaved feel abandoned. "My God, my God, why have you forsaken me?" Jesus cried from the cross. The miracle is realizing that death also brings empowerment. The discovery that love is stronger than death liberates.

I read a devotion that quoted the Reverend Henry Manning. I liked the quote and googled him. He was an Anglican priest in Sussex, England. In 1833, at age twenty-five, he married a woman named Caroline who was twenty-one. She died childless four years later. Manning then

became a celibate Roman Catholic cleric. Upon his death, a locket on a chain was found around the old man's neck. Inside the locket was a photograph of Caroline. Manning wrote of the dead, "Shall they love us the less because they now have power to love us more?"

This book is dedicated to those whom we see no more, but who love us all the more. It is about the countless ways their souls live on in ours, pushing through time. It is about how funerals teach me to live.

My sisters, Ginny and Cobey, and me on the stoop of Giles Apartments in 2015.

My dad on the same stoop in 1934.